PREFACE.

The studies which follow, the result of fifteen months' observation abroad, deal directly with the workers in all trades open to women, though, from causes explained in the opening chapter, less from the side of actual figures than the preceding volume, the material for which was gathered in New York. But as months have gone on, it has become plain that many minds are also at work, the majority on the statistical side of the question, and that the ethical one is that which demands no less attention. Both are essential to understanding and to effort in any practical direction, and this is recognized more and more as organization brings together for consultation the women who, having long felt deeply, are now learning to think and act effectually. These pages are for them, and mean simply another side-light on the labor question,—the question in which all other modern problems are tangled, and whose solving waits only the larger light whose first gleams are already plain to see.

HELEN CAMPBELL.

HEIDELBERG, GERMANY,
October, 1888.

CONTENTS.

CHAPTER I.

BOTH SIDES OF THE SEA.

With the ending of the set of studies among the working-women of New York, begun in the early autumn of 1886 and continued through several months of 1887, came the desire to know something of comparative conditions abroad, and thus be better able to answer questions constantly put, as to the actual status of women as workers, and of their probable future in these directions. There were many additional reasons for continuing a search, in itself a heart-sickening and utterly repellant task. One by one, the trades open to women, over ninety in number, had given in their returns, some of the higher order meaning good wages, steady work and some chance of bettering conditions. But with the great mass of workers, the wages had, from many causes, fallen below the point of subsistence, or kept so near it that advance was impossible, and the worker, even when fairly well trained, faced a practically hopeless future.

The search began with a bias against rather than for the worker, and the determination to do strictest justice to employer as well as employed. Long experience had taught what was to be expected from untrained, unskilled laborers, with no ambition or power to rise. Approaching the subject with the conviction that most of the evil admitted to exist must be the result of the worker's own defective training and inability to make the best and most of the wages received, it very soon became plain that, while this remained true, deeper causes were at work, and that unseen forces must be weighed and measured before just judgment could be possible. No denunciation of grasping employers answered the question why they grasped, and why men who in private relations showed warm hearts and the tenderest care for those nearest them became on the instant, when faced by this problem of labor, deaf and blind to the sorrow and struggle before them.

That the system was full of evils was freely admitted whenever facts were brought home and attention compelled. But the easy-going American temperament is certain that the wrong of to-day will easily become righted by to-morrow, and is profoundly sceptical as to the existence of any evil of which this is not true.

"It's pretty bad, yes, I know it's pretty bad," said one large employer of women, and his word was the word of many others. "But we're not to blame. I don't want to grind 'em down. It's the system that's wrong, and we are its victims. Competition gets worse and worse. Machinery is too much for humanity. I've been certain of that for a good while, and so, of course, these hands have to take the consequences."

Nothing better indicates the present status of the worker than this very phrase "hands." Not heads with brains that can think and plan, nor souls born to grow into fulness of life, but hands only; hands that can hold needle or grasp tool, or follow the order of the brain to which they are bond-servants, each pulse moving to the throb of the great engine which drives all together, but never guided by any will of brain or joy of soul in the task of the day. There has been a time in the story of mankind when hand and brain worked together. In every monument of the past on this English soil, even at the topmost point of springing arch or lofty pillar, is tracery and carving as careful and cunning as if all eyes were to see and judge it as the central point and test of the labor done. Has the nineteenth century, with its progress and its boast, no possibility of such work from any hand of man, and if not, where has the spirit that made it vanished, and what hope may men share of its return? Not one, if the day's work must mean labor in its most exhausting form; for many women, fourteen to sixteen hours at the sewing machine, the nerve-force supplied by rank tea, and the bit of bread eaten with it, the exhausted bodies falling at last on whatever may do duty for bed, with no hope that the rising sun will bring release from trial or any gleam of a better day.

With each week of the long search the outlook became more hopeless. Here was this army crowding into the great city, packed away in noisome tenement houses, ignorant, blind, stupid, incompetent in every fibre, and yet there as factors in the problem no man has yet solved. If this was civilization, better barbarism with its chance of sunshine and air, free movement and natural growth. What barbarism at its worst could hold such joyless, hopeless, profitless labor, or doom its victims to more lingering deaths? Admitting the almost impossibility of making them over, incased as they are in ignorance and prejudice, this is simply another count against the social order which has accepted such results as part of its story, and now looks on, speculating, wondering what had better be done about it.

The philanthropist has endeavored to answer the question, and sought out many devices for alleviation, struggling out at last to the conviction that prevention must be attempted, and pausing bewildered before the questions involved in prevention. For them there has been active and unceasing work, their brooms laboring as vainly as Mrs. Partington's against the rising tide of woe and want and fruitless toil, each wave only the forerunner of mightier and more destructive ones, while the world has gone its way, casting abundant contributions toward the workers, but denying that there was need for agitation or speculation as to where or how the next crest might break. There were men and women who sounded an alarm, and were in most cases either hooted for their pains, or set down as sentimentalists, newspaper philanthropists, fanatics, socialists,—any or all of the various titles bestowed freely by those who regard interference with any existing order of things as rank blasphemy.

Money has always been offered freely, but money always carries small power with it, save for temporary alleviation. The word of the poet who has sounded the depths of certain modern tendencies holds the truth for this also:—

> "Not that which we give, but what we share,
> For the gift without the giver is bare;
> Who bestows himself, with his alms feeds three,
> Himself, his hungering neighbor and me."

Yet it is the Anglo-Saxon conviction, owned by English and American in common, and unshaken though one should rise from the dead to arraign it, that what money would not do, cannot be done, and when money is rejected and the appeal made for personal consideration of the questions involved, there is impatient and instantaneous rejection of the responsibility. Evolution is supposed to have the matter in charge, and to deal with men in the manner best suited to their needs. If the ancient creed is still held and the worshipper repeats on Sunday: "I believe in one God, the Father Almighty, Maker of heaven and earth," he supplements it on Monday and all other days, till Sunday comes again, with the new version, the creed of to-day, formulated by a man who fights it from hour to hour:

"I believe in Father Mud, the Almighty Plastic;
And in Father Dollar, the Almighty Drastic."

It is because these men and women must be made to understand; because they must be reached and made to see and know what life may be counted worth living, and how far they are responsible for failure to make better ideals the ideal of every soul nearest them, that the story of the worker must be told over and over again till it has struck home. To seek out all phases of wretchedness and want, and bring them face to face with those who deny that such want is anything but a temporary, passing state, due to a little over-production and soon to end, is not a cheerful task, and it is made less so by those who, having never looked for themselves, pronounce all such statements either sensational or the work of a morbid and excited imagination. The majority decline to take time to see for themselves. The few who have done so need no further argument, and are ready to admit that no words can exaggerate, or, indeed, ever really tell in full the real wretchedness that is plain for all who will look. But, even with them, the conviction remains that it is, after all, a temporary state of things, and that all must very shortly come right.

Day by day, the desire has grown stronger to make plain the fact that this is a world-wide question, and one that must be answered. It is not for a city here and there, chiefly those where emigrants pour in, and so often, the mass of unskilled labor, always underpaid, and always near starvation. It is for the cities everywhere in the world of civilization, and because London includes the greatest numbers, these lines are written in London after many months of observation among workers on this side of the sea, and as the prelude to some record of what has been seen and heard, and must still be before the record ends, not only here, but in one or two representative cities on the continent. London, however, deserves and demands chief consideration, not only because it leads in numbers, but because our own conditions are, in many points, an inheritance which crossed the sea with the pilgrims, and is in every drop of Anglo-Saxon blood. If the glint of the sovereign and its clink in the pocket are the dearest sight and sound to British eyes and ears, America has equal affection for her dollars, in both countries alike chink and glint standing with most, for the best things life holds. It remains for us to see whether counteracting influences are stronger here than with us, and if the worker's chance is hampered more or less by the conditions that hedge in all labor. The merely statistical side of the question is left, as in the previous year's work, chiefly to those who deal only with this phase, though drawn upon wherever available or necessary. There is, however, small supply. Save in scattered trades-union reports, an occasional blue book, and here and there the work of a private investigator, like Mr. Charles Booth, there is nothing which has the value of our own reports from the various bureaus of labor. The subject has until now excited little interest or attention, save with a few political economists, and the band of agitators who are the disciples, not of things as they are, but things as they ought to be. One of the most admirable and well-officered organizations in New York, "The Workingwoman's Protective Union," which gave invaluable assistance last year, has only a small and feeble imitation in London, in the Woman's Protective Union, founded by Mrs. Peterson, and now under the admirable management of Miss Black, but still struggling for place and recognition.

Thus it will be seen that the work to be done here is necessarily more sketchy in character, though none the less taken from life in every detail, the aim in both cases being the same,—to give, as far as possible, the heart of the problem as it is seen by the worker, as well as by the eyes that may have larger interpretation for outward phases. The homes and daily lives of the workers are the best answers as to the comfort-producing power of wages, and in those homes we are to find what the wage can do, and what it fails to do, not alone for the East End, but for swarming lanes and courts in all this crowded London. The East End has by no means the monopoly, though novelists and writers of various orders have chosen it as the type of all wretchedness. But London wretchedness is very impartially distributed. Under the shadow of the beautiful abbey, and the towers of archiepiscopal Lambeth Palace; appearing suddenly in the midst of the great warehouses, and the press of traffic in the city itself, and thronging the streets of that borough road, over which the Canterbury pilgrims rode out on that immortal summer morning,—everywhere is the swarm of haggard, hungry humanity. No winter of any year London has known since the day when Roman walls still shut it in, has ever held sharper want or more sorrowful need. Trafalgar Square has suddenly become a world-wide synonym for the saddest sights a great city can ever have to show; and in Trafalgar Square our search shall begin, following one of the unemployed to the refuge open to her when work failed.

CHAPTER II.

IN TRAFALGAR SQUARE.

To the London mind nothing is more certain than that Trafalgar Square, which may be regarded as the real focus of the city, is unrivalled in situation and surroundings. "The finest site in Europe," one hears on every side, and there is reason for the faith. In spite of the fact that the National Gallery which it fronts is a singularly defective and unimpressive piece of architecture, it hardly weakens the impression, though the traveller facing it recalls inevitably a criticism made many years ago: "This unhappy structure may be said to have everything it ought not to have, and nothing which it ought to have. It possesses windows without glass, a cupola without size, a portico without height, pepper boxes without pepper, and the finest site in Europe without anything to show upon it."

In spite of all this, to which the pilgrim must at once agree, the Square itself, with the Nelson Pillar and the noble lions at its base, nobler for their very simplicity; its fountains and its outlook on the beautiful portico of St. Martin's, the busy Strand and the great buildings rising all about, is all that is claimed for it, and the traveller welcomes any chance that takes him through it. Treasures of art are at its back, and within short radius, every possibility of business or pleasure, embodied in magnificent hotels, theatres, warehouses, is for the throng that flows unceasingly through these main arteries of the city's life.

This is one phase of what may be seen in Trafalgar Square. But with early autumn and the shortening days and the steadily increasing pressure of that undercurrent of want and misery through which strange flotsam and jetsam come to the surface, one saw, on the long benches or crouched on the asphalt pavement, lines of men and women sitting silently, making no appeal to passers-by, but, as night fell, crouching lower in their thin garments or wrapping old placards or any sack or semblance of covering about them, losing memory in fitful sleep and waking with dawn to a hopeless day. This was the sight that Trafalgar Square had for those who passed through it, and who at last began to question, "Why is it? Who are they? They don't seem to beg. What does it mean?"

The Square presently overflowed, and in any and every sheltered spot the same silent lines lay down at night along the Thames Embankment, in any covered court or passage, men rushing with early dawn to fight for places at the dock gates, breaking arms or dislocating shoulders often in the struggle, and turning away with pale faces, as they saw the hoped-for chance given to a neighbor, to carry their tale to the hungry women whose office was to wait. The beggars pursued their usual course, but it was quite plain that these men and women had no affinity with them save in rags. Day by day the numbers swelled. "Who are they? What does it mean?" still sounded, and at last the right phrase was found, and the answer came: "They are the 'unemployed.' There is no longer any work to be had, and these people can neither get away nor find any means of living here."

For a time London would not believe its ears. There must be work, and so food for whoever was willing to work; but presently this cry silenced, and it became plain that somebody must do something.

Food was the first thought; and from the Limehouse district, and a refuge known as the Outcasts' Home, a great van loaded with loaves of bread came in two or three times a week, taking back to the refuge in the empty cart such few as could be induced to try its mercies. Coffee was also provided on a few occasions; and as the news spread by means of that mysterious telegraphy current in the begging fraternity, suddenly the Square overflowed with their kind; and who wanted to work and could not, and who wanted no work on any consideration, no man could determine.

With the story of this tangle, of the bewilderment and dismay for all alike, and the increasing despair of the unemployed, this chronicle has but indirectly to do. Trafalgar Square was emptied at last by means already familiar to all. Beggars skulked back to their hiding-places like wharf-rats to the rotten piles that shelter them; the unemployed dispersed also, showing themselves once more in the files that registered when the census of the unemployed was decided upon; and then, for the most part, were lost to public sight in the mass of general, every-day, to-be-expected wretchedness which makes up London below the surface.

mercifully removed by death. She was but twelve when her responsibility began, and it did not end when the mother came home, to be chiefly bedridden for such days as remained. The three little boys were all "mud-larks," that is, prowled along the river shore, picking up any odds and ends that could be sold to the rag-shop or for firewood, and their backs were scored with the strap which the father carried in his pocket and took out for his evening's occupation when he came.

The mother, sitting up in bed and knitting or crocheting for a small shop near by, fared no better than the rest, for Billy, who tried to stand between them, only infuriated the brute the more. The crisis came when he one night stole the strap from his father's pocket and cut it into pieces. Nelly, who was now earning fair wages, had long thought that her mother's life would be easier without them; and now, as Billy announced that he had done for himself and must run, she decided to run too.

"I told mother I'd have a bit of a room not far off," she said, "only where father wouldn't be likely to search us out, and I'd do for Billy and for her too what I could. She cried, but she saw it was best. Billy was just a bag of bones and all over strap marks. He'd have to mud-lark just the same, but he'd have more to eat and no beatings, and he'd always hung to me from the time he was born. So that is the way I did, and, bit by bit, I got a comfortable place, and had Billy in school, and kept us both, and did well. But then the wages began to go down, and every week they got lower till, where I'd earned twelve shillings a week sometimes, I was down to half and less than half that. I tried stitching for the sweaters a while, but I'd no machine, and they had more hands than they wanted everywhere, and I went back to the sacks. And at last they dismissed a lot too, and I went here and there and everywhere for another chance, and not one,—not one anywhere. I pawned everything, bit by bit, till we'd nothing left but some rags and straw to sleep upon, and the rent far behind; and then I went home when we were turned out, and that father took for his chance, and was worse than ever.

"And so, when there was no work anywhere, though I was ready for anything, I didn't care what, and I saw we were just taking the bread from mother's mouth (though it's little enough she wanted), then I told Billy to stay with her, and I went out and to the Square and sat down with the rest, and wondered if I ought to sit there and wait to be dead, or if I hadn't the right to do it quicker and just try the river. But I saw all those I was with just as bad off and worse, and some with babies, and so I didn't know what to do, but just to wait there. What can we do? They say the Queen is going to order work so that the men can get wages; but they don't say if she is going to do anything for the women. She's a woman; but then I suppose a Queen couldn't any way know, except by hearsay, that women really starve; and women do for men first anyhow. But I will work any way at anything, if only you'll find it for me to do—if only you will."

For one of the fifty-three thousand work and place have been found. For the rest is still the cry: "I will work any way at anything, if only you'll find it for me to do; if only you will."

———————————

CHAPTER III.

THE SWEATING SYSTEM IN GENERAL.

"History repeats itself," is a very hackneyed phrase, yet, for want of any better or more expressive one, must lead such words as are to be said on an old yet ever new evil; for it is just forty years ago, since the winter of 1847-1848 showed among the working men and women of England conditions analogous to those of the present, though on a far smaller scale. Acute distress prevailed then as now. Revolution was in the air, and what it might mean being far less plain to apprehensive minds than it is to-day, a London newspaper, desirous of knowing just what dangers were to be faced, sent a commissioner to investigate the actual conditions of the working classes, and published his reports from day to day. Then, for the first time, a new word came into circulation, and "sweating" became the synonym, which it has since remained, for a system of labor which means the maximum of profit for the employer and the minimum of wages for the employed. The term is hardly scientific, yet it is the only one recognized in the most scientific investigation thus far made. That of 1847-1848 did its work for the time, nor have its results wholly passed away. Charles Kingsley, young then and ardent, his soul stirred with longing to lighten all human suffering, took up the cause of the worker, and in his pamphlet "Cheap Clothes and Nasty," and later, in the powerful novel "Alton Locke," showed every phase of the system, then in its infancy, and, practically, entirely unknown on the other side of the Atlantic.

The results of this agitation became visible at once. Unions and Associations of various sorts among tailors and the one or two other trades to which the sweating system had applied, were organized and from year to year extended and perfected till it had come to be the popular conviction that, save in isolated cases here and there, the evil was to be found only among the foreign population, and even there, hedged in and shorn of its worst possibilities. This conviction remained and made part of the estimate of any complaints that now and then arose, and though the work of the organized charities, and of independent investigations here and there, demonstrated from year to year that it had increased steadily, its real scope was still unbelieved. Now, after forty years, the story tells itself again, this time in ways which cannot be set down as newspaper sensationalism or anybody's desire to make political capital. It is a Blue Book which holds the latest researches and conclusions, and Blue Books are not part of the popular reading, but are usually tucked away in government offices or libraries, to which the public has practically no access. A newspaper paragraph gives its readers the information that another report on this or that feature of public interest has been prepared and shelved for posterity, and there the matter ends.

In the present case public feeling and interest have been so stirred by the condition of unexampled misery and want among masses eager to work but with no work to be had, that the report has been called for and read and discussed to a degree unknown to any of its predecessors. While it gives results only in the most compact form and by no means compares with work like that of Mr. Charles Peck in his investigations for the New York Bureau of Statistics of Labor, it still holds a mass of information invaluable to all who are seeking light on the cause of present evils. As with us the system is closely a part of the manufacture of cheap clothing of every order, tailoring leading, and various other trades being included, furniture makers, strange to say, being among the chief sufferers in these.

With us the system is so clearly defined and so well known, at any rate in all our large centres of labor, that definition is hardly necessary. For England and America alike the sweater is simply a sub-contractor who, at home or in small workshops, undertakes to do work, which he in turn sublets to other contractors, or has done under his own eyes. The business had a simple and natural beginning, the journey-worker of fifty years ago taking home from his employers work to be done there either by himself or some member of his family. At this time it held decided advantages for both sides. The master-tailor was relieved from finding workshop accommodations with all the accompanying expense and from constant supervision of his work people, while good work was insured by the pride of the worker in his craft, as well as his desire not to lose a good connection. There was but the slightest subdivision of labor, each worker was able to make the garment from the beginning to the end, apprentices being employed on the least important parts.

Work of this order has no further place in the clothing trade, whether tailoring or general outfitting, save for the best order of clothing. Increase of population cheapened material, the introduction of machinery and the tremendous growth of the ready-made clothing trade are all responsible for the change. The minutest system of subdivided labor now rules here as in all trades. When a coat is in question, it is no longer the master-tailor, journeyman and apprentices who prepare it, but a legion of cutters, basters, machinists, pressers, fellers, button-hole, and general workers, who find the learning of any one alone of the branches an easy matter, and so rush into the trade, the fiercest and most incessant competition being the instant result.

In 1881 a census was taken in the East End of London which showed over fifteen thousand tailors at work, of whom more than nine thousand were women. The number of the latter at present is estimated to be about twelve thousand, much increase having been prevented by various causes, for which there is no room here. As the matter at present stands, every man and woman employed aims to become as fast as possible a sweater on his or her own account. For large employers this is not so easy; for the small ones nothing could be simpler, and here are the methods.

If the trade is an unfamiliar one, there is first the initiation by employment in a sweater's shop, and a few months, or even weeks, gives all the necessary facility. Then comes the question of workroom; and here it is only necessary to take the family room, and hire a sewing machine, which is for rent at two shillings and sixpence, or sixty cents, a week. To organize the establishment all that is necessary is a baster, a machinist, a presser, and two or three women-workers, one for button-holing, one for felling, and one for general work, carrying home, etc. The baster may be a skilled woman; the presser is always a man, the irons weighing from seven to eighteen pounds, and the work being of the most exhausting description, no man being able to continue it beyond eight or ten years at the utmost. The sweater-employer often begins by being his own presser, or his own baster; but as business increases his personal labor lessens. In the beginning his profits are extremely small, prices varying so that it is impossible to make any general table of rates. Even in the same branch of trade hardly any two persons are employed at the same rate, and the range of ability appears to vary with the wage paid, subdivision of labor being thus carried to its utmost limit, and the sections of the divisions already mentioned being again subdivided beyond further possibility. So tremendous is the competition for work that the sweaters are played off against each other by the contractors and sub-contractors, the result upon the workers below being as disastrous as the general effect of the system as a whole.

As one becomes familiar with the characteristics of the East End,—and this is only after long and persistent comings and goings in street and alley,—it is found that there are entire streets in Whitechapel or St. George's-in-the-East, the points where the tailoring trade seems to focus, in which almost every house contains one, and sometimes several, sweating establishments, managed usually by men, but now and then in the hands of women, though only for the cheapest forms of clothing. Here, precisely as in our own large cities, a room nine or ten feet square is heated by a coke fire for the presser's irons, and lighted at night by flaming gas-jets, six, eight, or even a dozen workers being crowded in this narrow space. But such crowding is worse here than with us, for reasons which affect also every form of cheap labor within doors. London, under its present arrangements, is simply an enormous smoke factory, and no quarter of its vast expanse is free from the plague of soot and smoke, forever flying, and leaving a coating of grime on every article owned or used, no matter how cared for. This is true for Belgravia as for the East End, and "blacks," as the flakes of soot are known, are eaten and drunk and breathed by everything that walks in London streets or breathes London air.

There is, then, not only the foulness engendered by human lungs breathing in the narrowest and most crowded of quarters, but the added foulness of dirt of every degree and order, overlaid and penetrated by this deposit of fine soot; the result a griminess that has no counterpart on the face of the earth. "Cheap clothes and nasty" did not end with Kingsley's time, and these garments, well made, and sold at a rate inconceivably low, are saturated with horrible emanations of every sort, and to the buyer who stops to think must carry an atmosphere that ends any satisfaction in the cheapness. Setting aside this phase as an intangible and, in part, sentimental ground for complaint, the fact that the cheapness depends also upon the number of hours given by the worker—whose day is never less than fourteen, and often eighteen, hours—should be sufficient to ban the whole trade. Even for this longest day there is no uniformity of price, and with articles identically the same the rate varies with different sweaters, the increasing competition accentuating these differences more and more. The sweater himself is more or less at the mercy of the contractor, who says to him: "Here are so many coats, at so much a coat. If you won't do them at the price, there are plenty that will."

Already well aware of this fact, the sweater, if the rate falls at all below his expectation, has simply to pursue the same course with the waiting worker in his shop, a slight turn of the screw, half a penny off here and a farthing there, bringing his own profit back to the rate he assumes as essential. There is no pressure from below to compel justice. For any rebellious worker a dozen stand waiting to fill the vacant place; and thus the wrong perpetuates itself, and the sweater, whose personal relation with those he employs may be of the friendliest, becomes tyrant and oppressor, not of his own will, but through sheer force of circumstances. Thus evils, which laws have not reached, increase from day to day. Inspectors are practically powerless, and the shameful system, degrading alike to employer and employed, grows by what it feeds on, and hangs over the East End, a pall blacker and fouler than the cloud of smoke and soot, also the result of man's folly, not to be lifted till human eyes see clearer what makes life worth living, and human hands are less weary with labor that profiteth not, but that deadens sense and soul alike.

This is the general view of the system as a whole. For the special there must still be a further word.

CHAPTER IV.

AMONG THE SWEATERS.

"'Nine tailors to make a man,' they say. Well, now if it takes that amount, and from some lots I've seen I should say it did, you've got to multiply by nine again if you count in the women. Bless your 'art!" and here, in his excitement, the inspector began to drop the *h*'s, which the Board School had taught him to hold to with painful tenacity. "Bless your 'art! a woman can't make a coat, and every tailor knows it, and that's one reason 'e beats 'er down and beats 'er down till 'ow she keeps the breath of life in the Lord only knows. Take the cheapest coat going and there's a knack to every seam that a woman don't catch. She's good for trousers and finishing, and she can't be matched for button-holes when she gives her mind to it, but a coat's beyond her. I've wondered a good bit over it. The women don't see it themselves, but now and again there's one that's up to every dodge but a coat seam, and she wants more money and couldn't be persuaded, no, not if Moses himself came to try it, that she isn't worth the same as the men. That's what I 'ear as I go, and I've been hup and down among 'em three years and over. Their dodges is beyond belief, not the women's,—poor souls! they're too ground down to 'ave mind enough left for dodges,—but the sweaters; Parliament's after 'em. There's enough, but ther's no man halive that I've seen that knows how to 'old a sweater to 'em. How's one or two inspectors to get through every sweating place in Whitechapel alone, let alone hall the East End? It's hup an' down an' hin and hout, and where you find 'em fair and square in a reg'lar shop, or in rooms plain to see, you'll find 'em in basements and backyards, and washhouses, and underground,—anywheres like so many rats, though, I'm blessed if I don't think the rats has the hadvantage. Now, the law says no working over hours, and I go along in the evening, about knocking-off time, and find everything all clear only a look in the sweater's heye that I know well enough. It means most likely that 'e's got 'is women locked up in a bedroom where the Parliament won't let me go, and that when my back's turned 'e'll 'ave 'em out, and grin in his sleeve at me and Parliament too. Or else 'e's agreed with 'em to come at six in the morning instead of eight. It's a twelve-hour day 'e's a right to, from eight to eight, but that way he make it fourteen and more, if I or some other inspector don't appear along.

"Now, suppose I drop down unexpected,—an' that's the way,—before I've made three calls, and likely nailed every one in the house for violation, it's down the street like lightening that the hinspector's after 'em. Then the women are 'ustled out anywhere, into the yard, or in a dust bin. Lift up 'most anything and you'd find a woman under it. I've caught 'em with their thimbles on, hot with sewing, and now they drop 'em into their pockets or anywhere. They'd lose a job if they peeped, and so there's never much to be done for 'em. But why a woman can't make a coat is what I study over. Did you ever think it out, ma'am? Is it their 'ands or their heyes that isn't hup to it?"

This position of the little inspector's problem must wait, though in it is involved that fatal want of training for either eye or hand which makes the lowest place the only one that the average needlewoman can fill. Their endurance equals that of the men, and often, in sudden presses of work, as for a foreign order, work has begun at seven o'clock on a morning and continued right on through the night and up to four or five of the next afternoon. The law demands an hour for dinner and half an hour for tea, but the first is halved or quartered, and the last taken between the stitches, but with no more stop than is necessary for swallowing. The penalties for violation of these acts are heavy and the inspectors work very thoroughly, various convictions having been obtained in 1886, the penalties varying from two pounds to ten pounds and costs. But the sweaters, though standing in terror of such possibility, have learned every device of evasion, and, as before stated, the women necessarily abet them for fear of losing work altogether.

Let us see now what the profit of the average sweater is likely to be, and then that of the workwoman, skilled and unskilled, taking our figures in every case from the Blue Book containing Mr. Burnett's report and confirmed by many workers. A small sweater in Brunswick Street employed a presser and a machinist, with two women for button-holes and felling, his business being the production of tunics for postmen. For each of these he received two shillings, or half a dollar a coat, which he considered a very good price. He paid his presser 4s. 6d. ($1.12) per day; his machinist 5s. ($1.25); his button-holer 2s. 6d. (60c.), from which she must find twist and thread; and the feller 1s. 3d. (30c.), a total of thirteen shillings threepence. For twelve coats he received twenty-four shillings, his own profit thus being ten shillings and ninepence ($2.68) for his own labor as baster and for finding thread, soap, coke, and machine. The hours were from seven in the morning to ten in the evening, less time not sufficing to finish the dozen coats, this bringing the rate of wages for the highest paid worker to 4½d., or nine cents an hour. For the small sweater the profit is slight, but each additional machine sends it up, till four or five mean a handsome return. If work is slack, he has another method of lessening expenses, and thus increasing profits, arranging matters so that all the work is done the three last days of the week, starting on a Thursday morning, for instance, and pressing the workers on for thirty-three to thirty-six hours at a stretch, calling this two days' work, and paying for it at this rate. If they work fractions of a day, eight hours is called a half and four a quarter day, and the men submit with the same patience as the women.

For the former this is in part a question of nationality, the sweater's workmen being made up chiefly of German and Polish Jews and the poorer foreign element. An English worker has generally learned the trade as a whole, and is secure of better place and pay; but a Polish Jew, a carpenter at home, goes at once into a sweater's shop, and after a few weeks has learned one branch of the trade, and is enrolled on the list of workers. For the women, however, there is a smaller proportion comparatively of foreigners. The poor Englishwoman, like the poor American, has no resource save her needle or some form of machine work. If ambitious, she learns button-holing, and in some cases makes as high as thirty shillings per week ($7.50). This, however, is only for the best paid work. Out of this she must find her own materials, which can never be less than two and sixpence (60c.). A woman of this order would do in a day twelve coats with six button-holes each, for the best class of work getting a penny a hole, or two cents. For commoner kinds the prices are a descending scale: three-quarters of a penny a hole, half a penny, eight holes for threepence, and the commonest kinds three holes for a penny. These are the rates for coats. For waistcoats the price is usually a penny for four button-holes, a skilled worker making sixteen in an hour. Many of these button-hole makers have become sweaters on their own account, and display quite as much ingenuity at cutting rates as the men at whose hands they may themselves have suffered.

For the machinists and fellers the rates vary. A good machinist may earn five shillings a day ($1.25), but this only in the busy season; the feller, at the best, can seldom go beyond three or four, and at the worst earns but six or eight per week; while learners and general hands make from two to six shillings a week, much of their time being spent in carrying work between the shops and the warehouses. Six shillings a week represents a purchasing power of about forty cents a day, half of which must be reserved for rent; and thus it will be seen that the English workwoman of the lower grade is in much the same condition as the American worker, hours, wages, and results being nearly identical. The Jewish women and girls represent a formidable element to contend with, as they are now coming over in great numbers, and the question has so organized itself that each falls almost at once into her own place, and works with machine-like regularity and efficiency.

In one of the houses in a narrow little street opening off from Whitechapel, were three women whose cases may be cited as representative ones. The first was a trouser machinist, and took her work from another woman, a sweater, who had it from city and other houses. She was paid threepence (6c.) a pair, and could do ten pairs a day, if she got up at six and worked till ten or eleven, which was her usual custom. In the next room was a woman who stitched very thick large trousers, for which she received fourpence a pair. She also had them from a woman who took them from a sub-contractor. She could make six and sometimes seven shillings a week, her rent being two shillings and sixpence. On the floor above was a waistcoat maker, who, when work was brisk, could earn eight and sometimes nine shillings a week; but who now, as work was slack, seldom went beyond six or seven. Out of this must be taken thread, which she got for eightpence a dozen. She worked for a small exporter in a street some ten minutes' walk away; but often had to spend two hours or more taking back her work and waiting for more to be given out. She fared better than some, however, as she knew women who many a time had had to lose five or six hours—"just so much bread out of their mouths."

"The work has to be passed," she said, "and there's never any doubt about mine, because I was bound to the trade, and my mother paid a pound for premium, and I worked three months for nothing—two months of that was clear gain to them, for I took to it and learned quick. But it's a starvation trade now, whatever it used to be."

"Why don't some of the best workers among you combine and get your work direct from the city house?"

"I've 'ad that in me mind, but there's never money enough. There's a deposit to be made for guarantee, and the machine-rent and all. No, there's never money enough. It's just keeping soul and body together, and barely that. We don't see butcher's meat half a dozen times a year; it's tea and bread, and you lose your relish for much of anything else, unless sprats maybe, or a taste of shrimps. I was in one workshop a while where there was over-hours always, and one night the inspector happened along after hours, and no word passed down, and the man turned me into the yard and turned off the gas; but I had to work two hours after he was gone. I'm better off than the woman in the next room. She makes children's suits—coats and knickerbockers—for ha'penny a piece, with tuppence for finishing, and her cotton to find; and, do 'er best, she won't make over four shillings and threepence a week, sometimes less. There's a mother and daughter next door that were bound to their trade for three months, and the daughter gave three months' work to learn it; but the most they make on children's suits is eight shillings and sixpence the two, and they work fifteen and sixteen hours a day."

This record of a house or two in Whitechapel is the record of street after street in working London. No trade into which the needle enters has escaped the system which has been perfected little by little till there is no loophole by which the lower order of worker can escape. The sweaters themselves are often kind-hearted men, ground by the system, but soon losing any sensitiveness; and the mass of eager applicants are constantly reinforced, not only by the steady pressure of emigrants of all nations, but by an influx from the country. In short, conditions are generally the same for London as New York, but intensified for the former by the enormous numbers, and the fact that outlying spaces do not mean a better chance. This problem of one great city is the problem of all; and in each and all the sweater stands as an integral part of modern civilization. Often far less guilty than he is counted to be, and often as much a sufferer as his workers from those above him, his mission has legitimate place only where ignorant and incompetent workers must be kept in order, and may well give place to factory labor. With skill comes organization and the power to claim better wages; and with both skilled labor and co-operation the sweater has no further place, and is transformed to foreman or superintendent. Till this is accomplished, the word must stand, as it does to-day, for all imaginable evil that can hedge about both worker and work.

CHAPTER V.

CHILD OF THE EAST END.

"What is it to be a lady?" The voice was the voice of a small and exceedingly grimy child, who held in her arms one still smaller and even grimier, known to the neighborhood as "Wemock's Orlando." Under ordinary circumstances, neither Wemock's nor anybody's youngest could have excited the least attention in Tower Hamlets where every doorway and passage swarms with children. But Orlando had the proud distinction of having spent three months of his short life in hospital, "summat wrong with his inside" having resulted from the kick of a drunken father who objected to the sight or sound of the children he had brought into the world, these at present numbering but seven, four having been mercifully removed from further dispensation of strap and fist and heavy boot.

Such sympathy as the over-worked drudges who constituted the wives of the neighborhood had to spare, had concentrated on Orlando, whose "inside" still continued wrong, and who, though almost three, had never been able to bear his weight on his feet, but became livid at once, if the experiment was tried,—a fact of perennial interest to the entire alley.

Wemock's fury at this state of things was something indescribable. A "casual" at the Docks, with the uncertainty of work which is the destruction of the casual laborer, he regarded the children as simply a species of investment, slow of making any return, but certain in the end. Up to five, say, they must be fed and housed somehow, but from five on a boy of any spirit ought to begin a career as mud-lark to graduate from it in time into anything for which this foundation had fitted him. The girls were less available, and he blessed his stars that there were but three, and cursed them as he reflected that Polly was tied hand and foot to Orlando, who persisted in living, and equally persisted in clinging to Polly, who mothered him more thoroughly than any previous Wemock had been.

Not that the actual mother had not some gleams of tenderness, at least for the babies. But life weighed heavily against any demonstration. She was simply a beast of burden, patient, and making small complaint, and adding to the intermittent family income in any way she could,—charing, tailoring, or sack-making when the machine was not in pawn, and standing in deadly terror of Wemock's fist. The casual, like most of the lower order of laborers, has small opinion of women as a class, and meets any remonstrance from them as to his habits with an unvarying formula.

"I'm yer 'usban', ain't I?" is the reply to request or objection alike, and "husband" by the casual is defined as "a man with a right to knock his woman down when he likes." This simplifies responsibility, and, being accepted with little or no question by the women, allows great latitude of action.

Wemock had learned that the strap was safer than a knock-down, however, as a dose of it overnight did not hinder his wife from crawling out of bed to prepare the breakfast and get to work, whereas a kick such as he preferred, had been known to disable her for a week, with inconvenient results as to his own dinners and suppers.

"It's the liquor as does it. 'E's peaceable enough when the liquor's out of 'im. But their 'ands comes so 'eavy. They don't know how 'eavy their 'ands comes." Thus Mrs. Wemock, standing in the doorway, for the moment holding Orlando, who resented his transfer with a subdued howl of grief, and looked anxiously down the alley toward Polly's retreating figure.

"'Ush now an' ma'll give him a winkle. Polly's gone for winkles. It's winkles we'll 'ave for supper, and a blessing it's there's one thing cheap and with some taste to it. A penny-'orth even, goes quite a way, but a penny-'orth ain't much when there's a child to each winkle an' may be two."

"The churchyard's been a better friend to me than to you," said a thin and haggard-looking woman, who had come across the street for a look at Orlando. "Out of my seventeen, there ain't but six left an' one o' them is in the Colonies. There's small call to wish 'em alive, when there's nought but sorrow ahead. If we was ladies I suppose it might all be different."

It was at this point that Polly's question was heard,—Polly, who had rushed back with the winkles and put the dish into her mother's hand and caught Orlando as if she had been separated from him hours instead of minutes. And Orlando in turn put his skinny little arms about her neck. Whatever might be wrong with his inside, the malady had not reached his heart, which beat only for Polly, his great dark eyes, hollow with suffering, fixing themselves on her face with a sort of adoration.

"A lady?" Mrs. Wemock said reflectively, eying her winkles, "there's more than one kind, Polly. A lady's mostly one that has nought to do but what she likes, and goes in a carriage for fear she'll soil her feet. But I've seen real ladies that thought on the poor, and was in and out among 'em. That kind is 'ard to find, Polly. I never knew but two an' they're both dead. It's them as has money, that's ladies, and them that hasn't—why they isn't."

"Then I can't be a lady," said Polly. "I heard Nelly Anderson say she meant to be a lady."

"Lord keep you from that kind!" said the mother hastily, with a significant look at her neighbor, which Polly did not fail to note and puzzle over. Tending Orlando gave her much time for puzzling. She was known as an "old fashioned" child, with ways quite her own, always to be depended upon, and confiding in no one but Orlando, who answered her in a language of his own.

"When I am a lady, we will go away somewhere together," Polly said. "I think I shall be a lady sometime, Orlando, and then we'll have good times. There are good times somewhere, only they don't get into the Buildings," and with a look at the sooty walls and the dirty passage she followed her mother slowly up the stairs, and took her three winkles and the big slice of bread and dripping, which she and Orlando were to share, into the corner. Orlando must be coaxed to eat, which was always a work of time, and before her own share had been swallowed, her father's step was on the stairs, and her mother turned round from the machine.

"Keep out of the way, Polly. 'E's taken too much, I know by the step of 'im, and 'e won't 'alf know what he's about."

Polly shrunk back. There was no time to get under the bed, which she often did, and she hugged Orlando close and waited fearfully. Both were silent, but she put her bread behind her. To see them eating sometimes enraged him, and he had been known to fling loaf and teapot both from the windows.

Both were on the table now, two or three slices spread with dripping for the younger boys who would presently come in. Wemock sat down, his hands in his pockets and his legs stretched out to their utmost length, and looked first at his wife who was stitching trousers, and then at Polly, whose eyes were fixed upon him.

"I'll teach you to look at me like that, you brat," he said, rising slowly.

"For the Lord's sake, Wemock!" his wife cried, for there was deeper mischief than usual in his tone. "Remember what you did to Orlando."

"I'll do for him again. I've 'ad enough of him always hunder foot. Out o' the way, you fool."

Polly looked toward the door. A beating for herself could be taken, but never for Orlando. Her mother had come between, and she saw her father strike her heavily, and then push her into the chair.

"Go on with your trousers," he said. "There's no money at the Docks, and these children eating me out of house and home. A man might be master of his own. Come 'ere. You won't, won't you? Then—"

There were oaths and a shriek from Orlando, on whom the strap had fallen; and then Polly, still holding him, rushed for the door, only to be caught back and held, while the heavy fist came down with cruel weight.

"Wemock's a bit worse than common," they said in the next room as the sounds began; but the shrieks in another moment had drawn every one in the Buildings, and the doorway filled with faces, no one volunteering, however, to interfere with the Briton's right to deal with his own as he will. He had flung Polly from him, and she lay on the floor unconscious and bleeding. Orlando had crept under the bed, and lay there paralyzed with terror; and the mother shrieked so loudly that the brute slunk back and seated himself again with attempted indifference.

"You've done for yourself this time," a neighbor said, and Wemock sprang up, too late to escape the policemen who had been brought by the sounds, not usual in broad daylight, and who suddenly had their hands upon him, while another stooped doubtfully over the child.

"She's alive," he said. "They take a deal to kill 'em, such do, but she'll need the 'ospital. Her arm's broke."

He lifted the arm as he spoke, and it fell limp, a cry of pain coming from the child, whose eyes had opened a moment and then closed with a look of death on the face. An ambulance was passing. Some one had been hurt on the Docks, where accidents are always happening, and was being carried to the hospital; and a neighbor ran down.

"It's best to do it sudden," she said, "or Orlando 'll never let her go or her mother either," and she hailed the ambulance driver, who objected to taking two, but agreed when he found it was only a child.

Polly came to herself at last, gasping with pain. A broken arm was the least of it. There was a broken rib as well, and bruises innumerable. But worse than any pain was the separation from Orlando, for whom Polly wailed, till, in despair, the nurse promised to speak to the surgeon and see if he might not be brought; and, satisfied with this hope, the child lay quiet and waited.

She was in a clean bed,—such a bed as she had never seen, and her soft dark eyes examined the nurse and all the strange surroundings in the intervals of pain. But fever came soon, and in long days of unconscious murmurings and tossings, all that was left of Polly's thin little frame wasted away.

"It is a hopeless case," the doctor said, "though after all with children you can never tell."

There came a day when Polly opened her eyes, quite conscious, and looked up once more at the nurse with the old appeal.

"I want Orlando. Where's Orlando?"

"He can't come," the nurse said, after a moment, in which she turned away.

"You promised," Polly said faintly.

"I know it," the nurse said. "He should come if he could, but he can't."

"Is he sick?" Polly said after a pause. "Did father hurt him?"

"Yes, he hurt him. He hurt him very much, but he can never hurt him any more. Orlando is dead."

Polly lay quite silent, nor did her face change as she heard the words; but a smile came presently, and her eyes lightened.

"You didn't know," she said. "Orlando has come. He is right here, and somebody is carrying him. He is putting out his arms."

The child had raised herself, and looked eagerly toward the foot of the bed, "She is bringing him to me. She says, 'Polly, you 're going to be a lady and never do what you don't want to any more.' I thought I should be a lady sometime, because I wanted to so much; but I didn't think it would be so soon. They won't know me in the Buildings. I'm going to be a lady, and never—"

Polly's eyes had closed. She fell back. What she had seen no man could know, but the smile stayed.

It was quite certain that something at least had come to her of what she wanted.

CHAPTER VI.

AMONG THE DRESSMAKERS.

"An Englishman's house is his castle," and an Englishwoman's no less, and both he and she ward off intruders with an energy inherited from the days when all men were fighters, and intensified by generations of practice. Even a government inspector is looked upon with deep disfavor as one result of the demoralization brought about by liberal and other loose ways of viewing public rights. The private, self-constituted one, it may then be judged rightly, is regarded as a meddlesome and pestilent busybody seeking knowledge which nobody should wish to obtain, and another illustration of what the nineteenth century is coming to. Various committees of inquiry, from the Organized Charities and from private bodies of workers, visit manufactories and industries in general, where women are employed, to make it evident that there is a desire to know how they fare. Why this wish has arisen, and why things are not allowed to remain as the fathers left them, are two questions at present distracting the British employer's mind, and likely, before the inquiry is ended, to distract it more, as, day by day, the numbers increase of those who persist in believing that they are in some degree their brothers' keepers,—a doctrine questioned ever since the story of time began. Obstacles of every nature are placed in the way of legalized inspection, and evasion and subterfuge, masterly enough to furnish a congress of diplomatists with ideas, are in daily practice. Years of experience make the inspector no less astute, and so the war goes on.

It will be seen then, what difficulties hedge about the private inquirer, who must go armed with every obtainable guarantee, and even then leave the field quite conscious that the informants are chuckling over a series of misleading statements, and that not much will be made of that case. So little organization exists among the workers themselves, and there is such deadly fear of losing a place that women and girls listen silently to statements, which they denounce afterwards as absolutely false. Natural as this is,—and it is one of the inevitable results of the system,—it is one of the worst obstacles in the way, not only of inquiry but any statements of results.

"Of course he lied or she lied," they say, "but don't for anything in the world let them know that we said so or that you know anything about it."

This injunction, which for the individual worker's sake must be scrupulously attended to, hampers not only inquiry but reform, and delays still further the attempts at organization made here and there. The system applied to dressmaking, our present topic, differs from anything known in America save in one of its phases, and merits some description, representing as it does some lingering remnant of the old apprentice system.

For the West End there is generally but one method. And here it may be said that the West End ignores absolutely any knowledge of what the East End methods may be. Between them there is a great gulf fixed, and the poorest apprentice of a West End house regards herself as infinitely superior to the mistress of an East End business. For this charmed region of the West, whether large or small, has spent years in building up a reputation, and this is a portion of the guarantee that goes with the worker, who has learned her trade under their auspices. It is a slow process,—so slow, that the system is not likely to be adopted by hasty Americans. In a first-class house in the West End, Oxford and Regent Streets having almost a monopoly of this title, the premium demanded for an apprentice is from forty to sixty pounds. This makes her what is known as an "indoor apprentice," and entitles her to board and lodgings for two years. Numbers are taken at once, beds are set close together in the rooms provided, and board is made of the cheapest, to prevent loss. This would seem very small, but add to it the fact, that the apprentice gives from twelve to sixteen hours a day of time and a year of time as assistant after the first probation is past, and it will be seen, that, even with no fee, the house is hardly likely to lose much.

The out-door apprentices pay usually ten pounds and board and lodge at home, but hours are the same; never less than twelve, and in the busy season, fourteen and sixteen. Tea is furnished them once a day, but no food, nor is there definite time for meals. In the case of in-door apprentices, with any rush of work, a supper is provided at ten, but the "out-doors" must bring such food as is needed. For them there is, as for learners, no pay for over-time; and the strain often costs the life of the country girls unused to confinement, who fall into quick consumption, induced not only by long hours of sitting bent over work, but by breathing air foul with the vile gas and want of ventilation, as well as, in many cases, the worst possible sanitary conditions. If the initiatory period is safely past, the apprentice becomes an "improver;" that is, she is allowed larger choice of work, looks on or even tries her own hand when draping is to be done, and if quick is shortly ranked as an assistant. With this stage comes a small wage. An out-door apprentice now earns from four to five shillings ($1.25) a week. The in-door one still receives only board, but soon graduates from second to first assistant, though the whole process requires not less than four years and is often made to cover six. As first assistant she is likely to have quarters slightly more comfortable than those of the apprentices, and she receives one pound a week,—often less, but never more. In case of over-time, this meaning anything over the twelve hours which is regarded as a day's work, various rates are paid. In the mourning department of one of the best known Oxford Street establishments, fourpence an hour is allowed. This rate is exceptionally high, being given because of the objection to evening work on black. The same house pays in the colored-suit department two and a half pence (5c.) an hour, and provides tea for the hands. Twopence an hour is given in several other houses, but for the majority nothing whatever.

The forewoman of one of these establishments began as an apprentice something over thirty years ago, and in giving these details and many others not included, expressed her own surprise that the amount of agitation as to over-time had produced so little tangible result.

"The houses are on the lookout, it's true," she said; "and each one is afraid of getting into the papers for violating the law, so the apprentice is looked out for a little better than she was in my time. I've worked many a time when there was a press of work—some sudden order to be filled—all night long. They gave us plenty of tea, a hot supper at ten, and something else at two, but they never paid a farthing, and it never came to one of us that we'd any right to ask it. There was one—a plucky little woman and a splendid hand. She was first assistant and we'd been going on like this a week one year. The girls fell fainting from their chairs. I did myself though I was used to it; and she stood up there at midnight, just before the manager came in and said, 'Girls, you've no right to take another stitch without pay. Who'll stand by me if I say so when Mr. B. comes in.' Not one spoke. 'Oh, you cowards!' she said. 'Not one? Then I'll speak for you.' Two rose up then and threw down their work. "Tis a burning shame,' says they. 'Say what you like!' Mr. B. was there before the words were out of their mouths, 'What's this? what's this?' he said. 'Not at work and the order to go out at noon?' 'Pay us then for double work, and not drive us like galley slaves,' said Mrs. Colman, standing very straight, 'I speak for myself and for the rest. We are going home.'

"The manager got purple. 'The first one that leaves this room, by G—, she'll never come back. What do you mean getting up this row, damn you?' 'I mean we're earning double, and ought to have it. Why shouldn't our pockets hold some of the profits on this order as well as yours?' 'Will you hush?' he says with his hand up as if he'd strike. 'No; not now, nor ever,' she says, she white and he purple, and out she walked; but none followed her. She never came back, and she was marked from that time, so she found it hard to get work. But she married again and went out to the Colonies, so she hadn't to fight longer. It's over-time now, as much as then, that is the greatest trouble. We had a Mutual Improvement Society when I was young, but oh, what hard work it was to go to it after nine in the evening and try to work, and it's hard work now, though people think you can be as brisk and wide awake after sewing twelve hours as if you'd been enjoying yourself."

In 1875 a few dressmakers, who had observed intelligently various organizations among men-tailors, boot-makers, etc., started an association of the "dressmakers, milliners, and mantua makers," designed for mutual benefit, a subscription of twopence per week being added to a small entrance fee. Rules were drawn up, one or two of which are given illustratively.

"Each person on joining is required to pay *one penny* for a copy of the rules, *one penny* for a card on which her payments will be entered, and *one shilling* entrance fee—but the last may be paid by instalments of fourpence each. After thirty years of age the entrance fee shall be 6*d*. extra for every additional ten years.

"Members not working in a business house, or not working in the above trades, can only claim sick benefits, but the usual death levy shall also be made for them.

"In case of death each member will be called upon to contribute *sixpence* to be expended as the deceased member may have directed.

"When a member is disabled by sickness (excepting in confinements), a notice must be signed by two members as vouchers to the secretary, who shall appoint the member living nearest to the sick member, with one member of the committee, to visit her weekly, and report to the committee before the allowance is paid, unless special circumstances require a relaxation of this rule. The committee may require a medical certificate."

Excellent as every provision was, and admirable work as was accomplished, the women, as is too often the case with women, lost mutual confidence, or could not be made to see the advantage of paying punctually, and the association dwindled down to a mere handful. In 1878 it reorganized, and its secretary, a working dressmaker, who learned her trade in a West End house, has labored in unwearied fashion to bring about some *esprit du corps* and though often baffled, speaks courageously still of the better time coming when women will have some sense of the value of organization. Her word confirms the facts gathered at many points in both East and West End. The East has reduced wages to starvation limit. A pound a week can still be earned in some houses at the West End—though fourteen or sixteen shillings is more usual; but for the other side, fourteen is still the highest point, and the scale descends to five and six—in one case to three and sixpence. Over hours, scanty food, exhaustion, wasting sickness, and death, the friend at last, when the weary days are done;—this is the day for most. The American worker has distinct advantages on her side, the long unpaid apprenticeship here having no counterpart there, and the frightfully long working day being also shortened. Many other disabilities are the same, but in this trade the advantage thus far is wholly for the American worker.

CHAPTER VII.

NELLY, A WEST-END MILLINER'S APPRENTICE.

What Polly had heard, listening silently, with "Wemock's Orlando" held close in her small arms, was quite true. Nelly Sanderson had determined to be a lady, and though uncertain as yet as to how it was to be brought about, felt that it must come. This she had made up her mind to when not much older than Polly, and the desire had grown with her. It was perfectly plain from the difference between her and Jim that Nature had meant her for something better than to stitch shirt-bodies endlessly. At twelve she had begun to do this, portions of two or three previous years having been spent in a Board School. Then her time for work and contribution to the family support had come. She was only a "feller," and took her weekly bundle of work from a woman, who, in turn, had it from another woman, who took it from a master-sweater, who dealt directly with the great city houses; and between them all, Nelly's wage was kept at the lowest point. But she did her work well, and was quick to a marvel; and her hope for the future carried her on through the monotonous days, broken only by her mother's scolding and Jim's insolence.

Jim was the typical East End loafer,—a bullet head, closely cropped; dull round eyes, and fat nose, also rounded; a thick neck, and fat cheeks, in which were plainly to be seen the overdoses of beer and spirits he had drunk since he was ten or twelve years old.

His mother had tried to keep him respectable. She had been a lady's maid; but that portion of her life was buried in mystery. It was only known she had come to Norwood Street when Nelly was a baby, and that very shortly Judkins, a young omnibus conductor, had fallen in love with her; and they had married, and taken rooms, and lived very comfortably till Jim was three or four years old. But the taste for liquor was too strong; and long days in fog and rain, chilled to the marrow under the swollen gray clouds of the London winter, were some excuse for the rush to the "public" at the end of each trip. The day's wages at last were all swallowed, and the wife, like a good proportion of workmen's wives, found herself chief bread-winner, and tried first one trade and then another, till Nelly's quick fingers grew serviceable.

Nelly was pretty,—more than pretty. Even Jim had moments of admiration; and the Buildings, in which several of her admirers lived, had seen unending fights as to who had the best right to take her out on Sundays. Her waving red-brown hair, her great eyes matching it in tint to a shade, her long black lashes and delicate brows, the low white forehead and clear pale cheeks,—anybody could see that these were far and away beyond any girl in the Buildings. The lips were too full, and the nose no particular shape; but the quick-moving, slender figure, like her mother's, and the delicate hands, which Nelly hated to soil, and kept as carefully as possible,—all these were indications over which the women, in conclave over tea and shrimps, shook their heads.

"'Er father was a gentleman, that's plain to see. She'll go the same way her mother did. I'd not 'ave one of my hown boys take up with her, not for no money."

This seemed the general verdict in the Buildings; and though Nelly sewed steadily all day and every day, the women still held to it, the men hotly contesting it, and family quarrels over the subject confirming the impression. Nelly worked on, however, unmoved by criticism or approval, spending all that could be saved from the housekeeping on the most stylish clothes to be found in Petticoat Lane market, and denying herself even in these for the sake of a little hoard, which accumulated, oh! so slowly since it had been broken into, once for a new feather for her little hat, once for a day's pleasuring at Greenwich; and Nelly resolved firmly it should never happen again.

One ambition filled her. This hateful East End must be left somehow. Somehow she must get to be the lady which she felt sure she ought to be. There were hints of this sometimes in her mother's talk; but it was plain that there was nobody to help her to this but herself. Already Jim drank more than his share. He was going the way of his father, dead years before in a drunken frolic; and the income made from the little shop her mother had opened, to teach him how to make a living, covered expenses, and not much more. Whatever was done for Nelly must be done by herself.

The way had opened, or begun to open, at Greenwich. A tall, delicate girl, who proved to be a milliner's apprentice, had taken a fancy to her, and given her her first real knowledge of the delights of West End life. She had nearly ended her apprenticeship, and would soon be a regular hand; and Nelly listened entranced to the description of marvellous hats and bonnets, and the people who tried them on, and looked disgustingly at her own.

"You've got a touch, I know," the new friend said approvingly. "You'd get on. Isn't there anybody to pay the premium for you?"

Nelly shook her head sorrowfully. "They couldn't do without me," she said. "There's mother and Jim, that won't try to earn anything, and I stitch now twelve hours a day. I'm off shirts, and on trousers. Trousers pay better. I've made eighteen shillings a week sometimes, but you must keep at it steady ahead for that."

"It's a pity," her companion said reflectively. "You'd learn quick. In three months you'd be an improver, and begin to earn, and then there's no knowing where you'd stop. You might get to be owner."

Nelly turned suddenly. She had felt for some time that some one was listening to them. They were on the boat, sitting on the central seat, back to back with a row of merry-makers; but this was some one different.

"I beg your pardon," he said; and Nelly flushed with pleasure at a tone no one had ever used before. "I have heard a little you were saying. I am interested in this question of wages, and very anxious to know more about it. I wish you would tell me what you know about this stitching."

He had come round to their side—a tall blond man of thirty, dressed in light gray, and a note-book in his hand. He was so serious and gentle that it was impossible to take offence, and very soon Nelly was telling him all she knew of prices in cheap clothing of every sort, and how the workers lived. She hated it all,—the grime and sordidness, the drunken men and screaming children; and her eyes flashed as she talked of it, and a flush came to her cheeks.

"You ought to have something better," the young man said presently, his eyes fixed upon her. "We must try to find something better."

Nelly's companion smiled significantly, but he did not notice it. Evidently he was unlike most of the gentlemen she had seen in the West End. Yet he certainly was a gentleman. He took them to a small restaurant when Nelly had answered all his questions, and they dined sumptuously, or so it seemed to them, and he sat by them and told stories, and entertained them generally all the way home.

"I shall go down the river next Sunday," he said low to Nelly as they landed. "Do you like to row? If you do, come to Chelsea to the Bridge, and we will try it from there."

This was the beginning, and for many weeks it meant simply that he pleased his æsthetic sense, as well as convinced himself that he was doing a good and righteous deed in making life brighter for an East End toiler. He had given her the premium, and Nelly, without any actual lie, had convinced her mother that the West End milliner was willing to take her for only two months of time given, and then begin wages. She brought out her own little fund, swollen by several shillings taken from one of the sovereigns given her, and proved that there was enough here to keep them till she began to earn wages again; and Mrs. Judkins allowed herself at last to be persuaded, feeling that a chance had come for the girl which must not be allowed to pass.

So Nelly's apprenticeship began. There was less rose-color than she had imagined. The hours were long, longer sometimes than her stitching had been, and many of the girls looked at her jealously. But Maria, her first friend, remained her friend. The two sat side by side, and Nelly caught the knack by instinct almost, and even in the first week or two caught a smile from Madame, who paused to consider the twist of a bow, quite Parisian in its effect, and said to herself that here was a hand who would prove valuable.

Nelly went home triumphant that night, and even her mother's sour face relaxed. She had taken up trouser-stitching again, forcing Jim to mind the shop, and saying to herself that the family fortunes were going to mend, and that Nelly would do it. Sundays were always free. Nobody questioned the girl. The young men in the Buildings and the street gave up pursuit. Plainly Nelly was not for them, but had found her proper place in the West End. They bowed sarcastically, and said, "'Ow's your Royal 'Ighness?" when they met; but Nelly hardly heeded them. The long wish had taken shape at last, —she was going to be a lady.

Summer ended. There was no more boating, but there were still long walks and excursions. The apprenticeship was over, and Nelly was now a regular hand, and farther advanced than many who had worked a year or two. She made good wages, often a pound a week. Her dress was all that such a shop demanded; her manner quieter every day.

"She's a lady, that's plain," Maria said; and Madame agreed with her, and took the girl more and more into favor. Nelly had a little room of her own now, next to Maria. She seldom went home, save to take money to her mother, and she never stayed long.

"It's best not," Mrs. Judkins said. "You're bound for something better, and you'll get it. This isn't your place. You're a bit pale, Nelly. It's the hours and the close room, I suppose?"

"Yes; it's the hours," Nelly said. "When there's a press, we're often kept on till nine or ten; but it's a good place."

She lingered to-day till Jim came in. Jim grew worse and worse, and she hurried away as she saw him swaggering toward the door; but there were tears in her eyes as she turned away. She passed her friend of the summer in Regent Street, and looked back for a moment. He had nodded, but was talking busily with a tall man, who eyed Nelly sharply. She had found that he lived in Chelsea, and was a literary man of some sort,—she hardly knew what,—and that his name was Stanley; beyond this she knew nothing. Some day he would make her a lady,—but when? There was need of haste. No one knew how great need.

Another month or two, the winter well upon them, and there came a day when Madame, who, as Nelly entered the workroom, had stopped for a moment and looked at her, first in surprise, then in furious anger, burst out upon her in words that scorched the ears to hear. No girl like that need sit down among decent girls. March, and never show her shameful face again.

Nelly rose silently, and took down her hat and shawl, and as silently went out, Madame's shrill voice still sounding. What should she do? The end was near. She could not go home. She must find Herbert, and tell him; but he would not be at home before night. She knew his number now, and how to find him. He must make it all right. She went into Hyde Park and walked about, and when she grew too cold, into a cocoa-room, and so the day wore away; and at five she took a Chelsea omnibus, and leaned back in the corner thinking what to say. The place was easily found, and she knocked, with her heart beating heavily, and her voice trembling as a maid opened the door and looked at her a moment.

"Come this way," she said, certain it must be a lady,—a visitor from the country, perhaps; and Nelly followed her into a back drawing-room, where a lady sat with a baby on her lap, and two or three children about her. A little boy ran forward, then stood still, his frightened, surprised eyes on Nelly's eyes, which were fixed upon him in terror.

"Whose is he?—whose?" she stammered.

"He is Herbert Stanley, junior," the lady said with a smile. "I'm Mrs. Stanley. Good Heaven! what is it?"

Nelly had stood for a moment, her hands reaching out blindly, the card with its name and number still in them.

"I must go," she said. "I must look for the real Herbert. This is another." She fell as the words ended, still holding the card tight; and when they had revived her, only shook her head as questions were asked. The boy stood looking at her with his father's eyes. There could be no doubt. Nelly rose and looked around; then, with no word to tell who she might be, went out into the night. She crossed the street, and stood hesitating; and as she stood a figure came swiftly down the street on the other side, and ran up the steps of the house she had left. There was no doubt any more; and with a long, bitter cry Nelly fled toward the river. There was no pause. She knew the way well, and if she had not, instinct would have led her, and did lead, through narrow alleys and turnings till the embankment was reached. No stop, even then.

CHAPTER VIII.

LONDON SHIRT-MAKERS.

Bloomsbury has a cheerful sound, and, like Hop Vine Garden and Violet Lane, and other titles no less reassuring, seems to promise a breath of something better than the soot-laden atmosphere offered by a London winter. But Hop Vine Garden is but a passage between a line of old buildings, and ends in a dark court and a small and dirty "public," the beer-pots of which hold the only suggestion of hops to be discovered. Violet Lane is given over to cat's-meat and sausage makers, the combination breeding painful suspicions in the seeker's mind, and Bloomsbury has long since ceased to own sight or smell of any growing thing.

But, in a gray and forlorn old group of houses known as Clark's Buildings, will be found, on certain evenings in the month, a little knot of women, each with open account-book, studying over small piles of pence and silver, and if their looks are any indication, drawing very little satisfaction from the operation. They are the secretaries of the little societies organized by the late Mrs. Patterson, who, like many other philanthropists, came to see that till the workers themselves were roused to the consciousness of necessity for union, but little could be accomplished for them. A few of the more intelligent, stirred by her deep earnestness, banded together twelve years ago, and organized a society known as "The Society of Women Employed in Shirt, Collar, and Under-linen Making;" and here may be found the few who have, from long and sharp experience, discovered the chief needs of workers in these trades. When outward conditions as they show themselves at present have been studied, when homes and hours and wages and all the details of the various branches have become familiar, it is to this dim little hall that one comes for a final puzzle over all that is wrong.

For it is all wrong; nor in any corner of working London, can any fact or figures make a right of the toil that is an old, old story; so old that there is even impatience if one tells it again. Numbers are unknown, each one who investigates giving a different result; but it is quite safe to say that five hundred thousand women live by the industries named in the society's title, not one of whom has ever received, or ever will receive, under the present system, a wage which goes beyond bare subsistence. Here, as in New York, or any other large city of the United States, the conditions governing the trade are much the same. The women, untrained and unskilled in every other direction, turn to these branches of sewing as the possibility for all, and scores wait for any and every chance of work from manufactory or small house. As with us, the work is chiefly put out, and necessarily at once arises the middle-man, or a gradation of middle-men, each of whom must have his profit, taken in every case—not from employer, but worker. The employer fixes his rates without reference to these. He is fighting, also, for subsistence, plus as many luxuries as can be added from the profits of his superior power over conditions. He may be, and often is, to those nearest him, kind, unselfish, eager for right. But the hands are "hands," and that is all; and the middle-man, of whom the very same statement may be true, deals with the hands with an equal obliviousness as to their connection with bodies and souls.

The original price per dozen of the garments made may be the highest in the market, but before the woman who works is reached there are often five, and sometimes more, transfers. Where workers are employed on the premises, they fare better, being paid by the piece. The minutest divisions of labor prevail, even more than with us—a shirt passing through many hands, the weekly wage differing for each. The "fitter," for instance, must be a skilled workwoman, the flatness and proper set of the shirt front depending upon correct fitting at the neck. For this fitting in West End houses, the fitter receives a penny a shirt, and can in a week fit twenty dozen—this meaning a pound a week. But slack seasons reduce the amount, so that often she earns but nine or ten shillings, her average for the year being about fourteen. For the grades below her the sum is proportionately less. The most thoroughly skilled hand in either shirt-making or under-linen has been known to make as high as twenty-eight shillings a week ($7.00), but this is phenomenal; nor, indeed, does any such possibility remain, prices having gone down steadily for some years. A pound a week for a woman, as has been stated elsewhere, is regarded even by just employers as all that can be required by the most exacting; and with this standard in mind, a fall of three or four shillings seems a matter of slight importance.

Taking the various industries in which women are employed, the needle, as usual, leading, and the shirt-makers being a large per cent of the number, there are in London nearly a million women, self-supporting and self-respecting, and often the sole dependence of a family. This excludes the numbers of thriftless and otherwise helpless poor whose work is variable, and who, at the best, can earn only the lowest possible wages as unskilled laborers. For the skilled ones, doing their best in long days of work, never less than twelve hours, the average earnings, after all chances of slack seasons and accidents have been taken into account, is never over ten shillings a week. It is worth while to consider what ten shillings can do.

The allowance per head for rations for the old people in the Whitechapel Workhouse, one of the best of its class, is according to the authorities, three shillings eleven pence (96c.) per week, the quantity falling somewhat below the amount which physiologists regard as necessary for an able-bodied adult. These supplies are purchased by contract, and thus a full third lower than the single buyer can command. But she has learned that appetite is not a point to be considered, and for the most part confines herself to tea and bread and butter, with a cheap relish now and then. Thus four shillings a week is made to cover food, and three shillings gives her a small back room. For such lights, fire, and washing as cannot be dispensed with, must be counted another shilling. Out of the remaining two shillings must come her twopence a week, if she belongs to any trades-union, leaving one shilling and ten-pence for clothes, holidays, amusements, saving, and the possible doctor's bill, a sum for the year, at the utmost, of from four pounds fifteen shillings and ninepence, or a trifle under twenty dollars. These women are, every one of them, past-mistresses in the art of doing without; and they do without with a patient courage, and often a cheerfulness, that is one of the most pathetic facts in their story. It is the established order of things. Why should they cry or make ado? Yet, as the workshop has its own education for men, and gives us the order known as the "intelligent workman," so it gives us also the no less intelligent workwoman, possessing not only the natural womanly gift of many resources, but the added power of just so much technical training as she may have received in her apprenticeship to her trade.

Miss Simcox, who has made a study of the whole question, comments on this, in an admirable article in one of the monthlies for 1887, emphasizing the fact that these women, fitted by experience and long training for larger work, must live permanently, with absolutely no outlook or chance of change, on the border-land of poverty and want. They know all the needs, all the failings of their own class. Many of them give time, after the long day's work is done, to attempts at organizing and to general missionary work among their order; and by such efforts the few and feeble unions among them have been kept alive. But vital statistics show what the end is where such double labor must be performed. These women who have character and intelligence, and unselfish desire to work for others, have an average "expectation of life" less by twenty years than that of the class who know the comfortable ease of middle-class life.

It is one of these workers who said not long ago, her words being put into the mouth of one of Mr. Besant's characters: "Ladies deliberately shut their eyes; they won't take trouble; they won't think; they like things about them to look smooth and comfortable; they will get things cheap if they can. *What do they care if the cheapness is got by starving women?* Who is killing this girl here? Bad food and hard work. Cheapness! What do the ladies care how many working girls are killed?"

The individual woman brought face to face with the woman dying from overwork, would undoubtedly care. But the workers are out of sight, hidden away in attic and basement, or the upper rooms of great manufactories. The bargains are plain to see, every counter loaded, every window filled. And so society, which will have its bargains, is practically in a conspiracy against the worker. The woman who spends on her cheapest dress the utmost sum which her working sister has for dress, amusements, culture, and saving, preaches thrift, and it is certain the working classes would be better off if they had learned to save. Small wonder that the workers doubt them and their professed friendship, and that the breach widens day by day between classes and masses, bridged only by the work of those who, like the workers in the Women's Provident League, know that it is to the rich that the need for industry must be preached, not to the poor. Organization holds education for both, and it is now quite possible to know something of the methods of prominent firms with their workwomen, and to shun those which refuse to consider the questions of over-time, of unsanitary workrooms, of unjust fines and reductions, and the thousand ways of emptying some portion of the workwoman's purse into that of the employer.

CHAPTER IX.

THE TALE OF A BARROW.

If the West End knows not the East End, save as philanthropy and Mr. Walter Besant have compelled it, much less does it know Leather Lane, a remnant of old London, now given over chiefly to Italians, and thus a little more picturesquely dirty than in its primal state of pure English grime. The eager business man hurrying down "that part of Holborn christened High," is as little aware of the neighborhood of Leather Lane and what it stands for, as the New Yorker on Broadway is of Mulberry Street and the Great Bend. For either or both, entrance is entrance into a world quite unknown to decorous respectability, and, if one looks aright, as full of wonders and discoveries as other unknown countries under our feet. Out of Leather Lane, with its ancient houses swarming with inhabitants and in all stages of decay and foulness, open other lanes as unsavory, through which the costers drive their barrows, chaffering with dishevelled women, who bear a black eye or other token that the British husband has been exercising his rights, and who find bargaining for a bunch of turnips or a head of cabbage an exhilarating change.

There were many costers and many barrows, but among them all hardly one so popular as "old Widgeon," who had been in the business forty years; and as he had chosen to remain a bachelor, an absolutely unheard-of state of things, he was an object of deepest interest to every woman in Leather Lane and its purlieus. It was always possible that he might change his mind; and from the oldest inhabitant down to the child just beginning to ask questions, there was always a sense of expectation where Widgeon was concerned. He, in the meantime, did his day's work contentedly, had a quick eye for all trouble, and in such cases was sure to give overweight, or even to let the heavy penny or two fall accidentally into the purchase. His donkey had something the same expression of patient good-humored receptivity. The children climbed over the barrow and even on the donkey's back, and though Widgeon made great feint of driving them off with a very stubby whip, they knew well that it would always just miss them, and returned day after day undismayed. He "did for himself" in a garret in a dark little house, up a darker court; and here it was popularly supposed he had hidden the gains of all these forty years. They might be there or in the donkey's stable, but they were somewhere, and then came the question, who would have them when he died?

To these speculations Nan listened silently, in the pauses of the machines on which her mother and three other women stitched trousers. Nothing was expected of her but to mind the baby, to see that the fire kept in, just smouldering, and that there was always hot water enough for the tea. On the days when they all stitched she fared well enough; but when she had carried home the work, and received the money, there was a day, sometimes two or three, in which gin ruled, and the women first shouted and sang songs, and at last lay about the floor in every stage of drunkenness. Gradually chances for work slipped away; the machines were given up, and the partnership of workers dissolved, and at twelve, Nan and the baby were beggars and the mother in prison for aggravated assault on a neighbor. She died there, and thus settled one problem, and now came the other, how was Nan to live?

Old Widgeon answered this question. They had always been good friends from the day he had seen her standing, holding the baby, crippled and hopelessly deformed from its birth. His barrow was almost empty, and the donkey pointing his long ears toward the stable.

"Get in," he said, "an' I'll give you a bit of a ride," and Nan, speechless with joy, climbed in and was driven to the stable, and once there, watched the unharnessing and received some stray oranges as she finally turned away. From that day old Widgeon became her patron saint. She had shot up into a tall girl, shrinking from those about her, and absorbed chiefly in the crooked little figure, still "the baby;" but tall as she might be, she was barely twelve, and how should she hire a machine and pay room rent and live?

Widgeon settled all that.

"You know how to stitch away at them trousers?" he had said, and Nan nodded.

"Then I'll see you through the first week or two," he said; "but, mind! don't you whisper it, or I'll 'ave hevery distressed female in the court down on me, and there's enough hof 'em now."

Nan nodded again, but he saw the tears in her eyes, and regarded words as quite unnecessary. The sweater asked no questions when she came for a bundle of work, nor did she tell him that she alone was now responsible. She had learned to stitch. Skill came with practice, and she might as well have such slight advantage as arose from being her mother's messenger.

So Nan's independent life began, and so it went on. She grew no taller, but did grow older, her silent gravity making her seem older still. It was hard work. She had never liked tea, and she loathed the sight and smell of either beer or spirits, old experience having made them hateful. Thus she had none of the nervous stimulant which keeps up the ordinary worker, and with small knowledge of any cookery but boiling potatoes and turnips, and frying bacon or sprats, fared worse than her companions. But she had learned to live on very little. She stitched steadily all day and every day, gaining more and more skill, but never able to earn more than fourteen shillings a week. Prices went down steadily. At fourteen shillings she could live, and had managed even not only to pay Widgeon but to pick up some "bits of things." She was like her father, the old people in the alley said. He had been a silent, decent, hard-working man, who died broken-hearted at the turn his wife took for drink. Nan had his patience and his faithfulness; and Johnny, who crawled about the room, and could light a fire and do some odds and ends of house-keeping, was like her, and saved her much time as he grew older, but hardly any bigger. He had even learned to fry sprats, and to sing, in a high, cracked, little voice, a song known throughout the alley:—

> "Oh, 'tis my delight of a Friday night,
>   When sprats they isn't dear,
> To fry a couple o' dozen or so
>   Upon a fire clear."

There are many verses of this ditty, all ending with the chorus:—

> "Oh, 'tis my delight of a Friday night!"

and Johnny varied the facts ingeniously, and shouted "bacon," or anything else that would fry, well pleased at his own ingenuity.

"He was 'wanting.' Nan might better put him away in some asylum," the neighbors said; but Nan paid no attention. He was all she had, and he was much better worth working for than herself, and so she went on.

Old Widgeon had been spending the evening with them. Nan had stitched on as she must; for prices had gone down again, and she was earning but nine shillings a week. Widgeon seldom said much. He held Johnny on his knee, and now and then looked at Nan.

"It's a dog's life," he said at last. "It's far worse than a dog's. You'd be better off going with a barrow, Nan. I'm a good mind to leave you mine, Nan. You'd get a bit of air, then, and you'd make—well, a good bit more than you do now."

Widgeon had checked himself suddenly. Nobody knew what the weekly gain might be, but people put it as high as three pounds; and this was fabulous wealth.

"I've thought of it," Nan said. "I've thought of it ever since that day you rode me and Johnny in the barrow. Do you mind? The donkey knows me now, I think. He's a wise one."

"Ay, he's a wise one," the old man said. "Donkeys is wiser than folks think." He put Johnny down suddenly, and sat looking at him strangely; but Nan did not see. The machine whirred on, but it stopped suddenly as Johnny cried out. Widgeon had slipped silently from his chair; his eyes were open, but he did not seem to see her, and he was breathing heavily. Nan ran into the passage and called an old neighbor, and the two together, using all their strength, managed to get him to the bed.

"It's a stroke," the woman said. "Lord love you, what'll you do? He can't stay here. He'd better be sent to 'ospital."

"I'll be 'anged first," said old Widgeon, who had opened his eyes suddenly and looked at them both. "I was a bit queer, but I'm right enough now. Who talks about 'ospitals?"

He tried to move and his face changed.

"I'm a bit queer yet," he said, "but it'll pass; it'll pass. Nan, you'll not mind my being in your way for a night. There's money in me pocket. Maybe there's another room to be 'ad."

"There's a bit of a one off me own that was me John's, an' him only gone yesterday," said the woman eagerly; "an' a bed an' all, an' openin' right off of this. The door's behind that press. It's one with this, an' the two belongs together, an' for two an' six a week without, an' three an' six with all that's in it, it's for anybody that wants it."

"I'll take it a week," said old Widgeon, "but I'll not want the use of it more than this night. I'm a bit queer now, but it'll pass; it'll pass."

The week went, but old Widgeon was still "a bit queer;" and the doctor, who was at last called in, said that he was likely to remain so. One side was paralyzed. It might lessen, but would never recover entirely. He would have to be looked out for. This was his daughter? She must understand that he needed care, and would not be able to work any more.

Old Widgeon heard him in silence, and then turned his face to the wall, and for hours made no sign. When he spoke at last, it was in his usual tone.

"I thought to end my days in the free air," he said, "but that ain't to be. And I'm thinking the stroke's come to do you a good turn, Nan. There's the donkey and the barrow, and everybody knowing it as well as they know me. I'll send you to my man in Covent Garden. He's a fair 'un. He don't cheat. He'll do well by you, an' you shall drive the barrow and see what you make of it. We'll be partners, Nan. You look out for me a bit, an' I'll teach you the business and 'ave an heye to Johnny. What do you say? Will you try it? It'll break me 'art if that donkey and barrow goes to hanybody that'll make light of 'em hand habuse 'em. There hain't such another donkey and barrow in all London, and you're one that knows it, Nan."

"Yes, I know it," Nan said. "You ought to know, if you think I could do it."

"There's nought that can't be done if you sets your mind well to it," said old Widgeon. "And now, Nan, 'ere's the key, and you get Billy just by the stable there to move my bits o' things over here. That court's no place for you, an' there's more light here. Billy's a good 'un. He'll 'elp you when you need it."

This is the story of the fresh-faced, serious young woman who drives a donkey-barrow through certain quiet streets in northwest London, and has a regular line of customers, who find her wares, straight from Covent Garden, exactly what she represents. Health and strength have come with the new work, and though it has its hardships, they are as nothing compared with the deadly, monotonous labor at the machine. Johnny, too, shares the benefit, and holds the reins or makes change, at least once or twice a week, while old Widgeon, a little more helpless, but otherwise the same, regards his "stroke" as a providential interposition on Nan's behalf, and Nan herself as better than any daughter.

"I've all the good of a child, and none o' the hups hand downs o' the married state," he chuckles; "hand so, whatever you think, I'm lucky to the hend."

CHAPTER X.

STREET TRADES AMONG WOMEN.

"With hall the click there is to a woman's tongue you'd think she could 'patter' with the best of the men, but, Lor' bless you! a woman can't 'patter' any more'n she can make a coat, or sweep a chimley. And why she can't beats me, and neither I nor nobody knows."

"To patter" is a verb conjugated daily by the street seller of any pretensions. The coster needs less of it than most vendors, his wares speaking for themselves; but the general seller of small-wares, bootlaces, toys, children's books, and what not, must have a natural gift, or acquire it as fast as possible. To patter is to rattle off with incredible swiftness and fluency, not only recommendations of the goods themselves, but any side thoughts that occur; and often a street-seller is practically a humorous lecturer, a student of men and morals, and gives the result in shrewd sentences well worth listening to. Half a dozen derivations are assigned to the word, one being that it comes from the rattled off *paternosters* of the devout but hasty Catholic, who says as many as possible in a given space of time. Be this as it may, it is quite true that pattering is an essential feature of any specially successful street-calling, and equally true that no woman has yet appeared who possesses the gift.

In spite of this nearly fatal deficiency, innumerable women pursue street trades, and, notwithstanding exposure and privation and the scantiest of earnings, have every advantage over their sisters of the needle. Rheumatism, born of bad diet and the penetrating rawness and fogs of eight months of the English year, is their chief enemy; but as a whole they are a strong, hardy, and healthy set of workers, who shudder at the thought of bending all day over machine or needle, and thank the fate that first turned them toward a street-calling. So conservative, however, is working England, that the needlewoman, even at starvation point, feels herself superior to a street-seller; and the latter is quite conscious of this feeling, and resents it accordingly. With many the adoption of such employment is the result of accident, and the women in it divide naturally into four classes: (1) The wives of street-sellers; (2) Mechanics, or laborers' wives who go out street-selling while their husbands are at work, in order to swell the family income; (3) The widows of former street-sellers; (4) Single women.

Trades that necessitate pushing a heavy barrow, and, indeed, most of those involving the carrying of heavy weights, are in the hands of men, and also the more skilled trades, such as the selling of books or stationery,—in short, the business in which patter is demanded. Occasionally there is a partnership, and man and wife carry on the same trade, she aiding him with his barrow, but for the most part they choose different occupations. In the case of one man in Whitechapel who worked for a sweater; the wife sold water-cresses morning and evening, while the wife of a bobbin turner had taken to small-wares, shoe-laces, etc. as a help. Both tailor and turner declared that, if things went on as they were at present, they should take to the streets also; for earnings were less and less, and they were "treated like dirt, and worse."

The women whose trades have been noted are dealers in fish, shrimps, and winkles, and sometimes oysters, fruit, and vegetables,—fruit predominating, orange-women and girls being as much a feature of London street life as in the days of pretty Nelly Gwynne. Sheep-trotters, too, are given over to women, with rice-milk, which is a favorite street-dainty, requiring a good deal of preparation; they sell curds and whey, and now and then, though very seldom, they have a coffee or elder-wine stand, the latter being sold hot and spiced, as a preventive of rheumatism and chill. To these sales they add fire-screens and ornaments (the English grate in summer being filled with every order of paper ornamentation), laces, millinery, cut flowers, boot and corset laces, and small-wares of every description, including wash-leathers, dressed and undressed dolls, and every variety of knitted articles, mittens, cuffs, socks, etc.

It will be seen that the range in street trades is far wider for the English than for the American woman, to whom it would almost never occur as a possible means of livelihood. But London holds several thousands of these women, a large proportion Irish, it is true, with a mixture of other nationalities, but English still predominating. The Irishwoman is more fluent, and can even patter in slight degree, but has less intelligence, and confines herself to the lower order of trades. For both Irish and English there is the same deep-seated horror of the workhouse. All winter a young Irishwoman has sat at the corner of a little street opening from the Commercial Road, a basket of apples at her side, and her thin garments no protection against the fearful chill of fog and mist. She had come to London, hoping to find a brother and go over with him to America; but no trace of him could be discovered, and so she borrowed a shilling and became an apple-seller.

"God knows," she said, "I'd be better off in the house [workhouse], for it's half dead I am entirely; but I'd rather live on twopence a day than come to that."

Practically she was living on very little more. An aunt, also a street-seller, had taken her in. She rented a small room near by, for which they paid two shillings a week, their whole expenses averaging sixpence each a day. Naturally they were half starved; but they preferred this to "the house," and no one who has examined these retreats can blame them.

It is the poor who chiefly patronize these street-sellers, and they swarm where the poor are massed. The "Borough," on the Surrey side of the river, with its innumerable little streets and lanes, each more wretched than the last, has hundreds of them, no less than the better-known East End. Leather Lane, one of the most crowded and distinctive of the quarters of the poor, though comparatively little known, has also its network of alleys and courts opening from it, and is one of the most crowded markets in the city, rivalling even Petticoat Lane. The latter, whose time-honored name has foolishly been changed to Middlesex Street, is an old-clothes market, and presents one of the most extraordinary sights in London; but the trade is chiefly in the hands of men, though their wives usually act as assistants and determine the quality of a garment till the masculine sense has been educated up to the proper point. Any very small, very old, and very dirty street at any point has its proportion of street-sellers, whose dark, grimy, comfortless rooms are their refuge at night. Other rooms of a better order are occupied, it may be, by some relative or child to be supported; and higher still rank those that are counted homes, where husband and wife meet when the day's work is done.

Like the needlewomen, the diet of the majority is meagre and poor to a degree. The Irishwoman is much more ready to try to make the meal hot and relishable than the Englishwoman, though even she confines herself to cheap fish and potatoes, herring or plaice at two a penny.

A quiet, very respectable looking woman, the widow of a coster, sold cakes of blacking and small-wares, and gave her view of this phase of the question.

"It's cheaper, their way of doing. Oh, yes, but not so livening. I could live cheaper on fish and potatoes than tea and bread and butter; but that ain't it. They're more trouble, an' when you've been on your legs all day, an' get to your bit of a home for a cup of tea, you want a bit of rest, and you can't be cooking and fussing with fish. There's always a neighbor to give you a jug of boiling water, if you've no time for fire, or it's summer, and tea livens you up a bit where a herring won't. I take mine without milk, and like it better without, and often I don't have butter on me bread. But I get along, and, please God, I'll be able to keep out of the 'house' to the end."

The married women fare better. The men decline to be put off with bread and tea, and the cook-shops and cheap markets help them to what they call good living. They buy "good block ornaments," that is, small pieces of meat, discolored but not dirty nor tainted, which are set out for sale on the butcher's block. Tripe and cowheel are regarded as dainties, and there is the whole range of mysterious English preparations of questionable meat, from sausage and polonies to saveloys and cheap pies. Soup can be had, pea or eel, at two or three pence a pint, and beer, an essential to most of them, is "threepence a pot [quart] in your own jugs." A savory dinner or supper is, therefore, an easy matter, and the English worker fares better in this respect than the American, for whom there is much less provision in the way of cheap food and cook-shops. In fact the last are almost unknown with us, the cheap restaurant by no means taking their place. Even with bread and tea alone, there is a good deal more nourishment, since English bread is never allowed to rise to the over-lightness which appears an essential to the American buyer. The law with English breads and cakes of whatever nature appears to be to work in all the flour the dough can hold, and pudding must be a slab, and bread compact and dense to satisfy the English palate. Dripping is the substitute for butter, and the children eat the slice of bread and dripping contentedly. Fat of any sort is in demand, the piercing rawness of an English winter seeming to call for heating food no less than that of the Esquimaux for its rations of blubber and tallow. But the majority of the women leave dripping for the children, and if a scrap of butter cannot be had, rest contented with bread and tea, and an occasional pint of beer. For workingwomen as a class, however, there is much less indulgence in this than is supposed. To the men it is as essential as the daily meals, and the women regard it in the same way. "We do well enough with our tea, but a man must have his pint," they say; and this principle is applied to the children, the girls standing by while the boys take their turn at the "pot of mild."

This for the best order of workers. Below this line are all grades of indulgence ending with the woman who earns just enough for the measure of gin that will give her a day or an hour of unconsciousness and freedom from any human claim. But the pressure of numbers and of competing workers compels soberness, the steadiest and most capable being barely able to secure subsistence, while below them is every conceivable phase of want and struggle, more sharply defined and with less possibility of remedy than anything found in the approximate conditions on American soil.

CHAPTER XI.

LONDON SHOP-GIRLS.

"It's the ladies that's in the way, mum. Once get a lady to think that a girl isn't idling because she's sitting down, and the battle's won. But a lady comes into a shop blacker 'n midnight if every soul in it isn't on their feet and springing to serve her. I've got seats, but, bless you! my trade 'd be ruined if the girls used them much. 'Tisn't that I'm not willing, and me brother as well. It's the customers, the lady customers, that wouldn't stand it. Its them that you've got to talk to."

Once more it is a woman who is apparently woman's worst enemy, and London sins far more heavily in this respect than New York, and for a very obvious reason, that of sharply defined lines of caste, and the necessity of emphasizing them felt by all whose position does not speak for itself. A "born lady" on entering a shop where women clerks were sitting, might realize that from eleven to fourteen hours' service daily might well be punctuated by a few moments on the bits of board pushed in between boxes, which do duty for seats, and be glad that an opportunity had been improved. Not so the wife of the prosperous butcher or baker or candlestick maker, rejoicing, it may be, in the first appearance in plush and silk, and bent upon making it as impressive as possible. To her, obsequiousness is the first essential of any dealing with the order from which she is emerging; and her custom will go to the shop where its outward tokens are most profuse. A clerk found sitting is simply embodied impertinence, and the floor manager who allows it an offender against every law of propriety; and thus it happens that seats are slipped out of sight, and exhausted women smile and ask, as the purchase is made, "And what is the next pleasure?" in a tone that makes the American hearer cringe for the abject humility that is the first condition of success as seller.

Even the best shops are not exempt from this, and as one passes from west to east the ratio increases, culminating in the oily glibness of the bargain-loving Jew, and his no less bargain-loving London brother of Whitechapel, or any other district unknown to fashion.

This, however, is a merely outward phase. The actual wrongs of the system lie deeper, but are soon as apparent. For the shop-girl, as for the needlewoman or general worker of any description whatsoever, over-time is the standing difficulty, and a grievance almost impossible to redress. That an act of parliament forbids the employment of any young person under eighteen more than eleven hours a day, makes small difference. Inspectors cannot be everywhere at once, and violations are the rule. In fact, the law is a dead letter, and the employer who finds himself suddenly arraigned for violation is as indignant as if no responsibility rested upon him. A committee has for many months been doing self-elected work in this direction, registering the names of shops where over-hours are demanded, informing the clerks of the law and its bearings, and urging them to make formal complaint. The same difficulty confronts them here as in the attempts to reduce over-time for tailoresses and general needlewomen—the fear of the workers themselves that any complaint will involve the losing of the situation; and thus silent submission is the rule for all, any revolt bringing upon them instant discharge.

In a prolonged inquiry into the condition of shop-girls in both the West and East End, the needs to be met first of all summed themselves up in four: (1) more seats and far more liberty in the use of them; (2) better arrangements for midday dinner—on the premises if possible, the girls now losing much of the hour in a hurried rush to the nearest eatinghouse; (3) with this, some regularity as to time for dinner, this being left at present to the caprice of the manager, who both delays and shortens time; (4) much greater care in the selection of managers. A fifth point might well be added, that of a free afternoon each week. This has been given by a few London firms, and has worked well in the added efficiency and interest of the girls, but by the majority, is regarded as a wild and very useless innovation.

The first point is often considered as settled, yet for both sides of the sea is actually in much the same case. Seats are kept out of sight, and for the majority of both sellers and buyers, there is the smallest comprehension of the strain of continuous standing, or its final effect. It is the popular conviction that women "get used to it," and to a certain extent this is true, the strong and robust adjusting themselves to the conditions required. But the majority must spend the larger portion of the week's earnings on the neat clothing required by the position, and to accomplish this they go underfed to a degree that is half starvation. It is this latter division of shop girls who suffer, not only from varicose veins brought on by long standing, but from many other diseases, the result of the same cause; yet, till women, who come as purchasers to the shops where women are employed, realize and remember this, reform under this head is practically impossible. The employer knows that, even if a few protest against the custom, his trade would suffer were it done away with; and thus buyer and seller form a combination against which revolt is impossible.

The inquiry brought one fact to light, which, so far as I know, has as yet no counterpart in the United States, and this is, that in certain West End shops every girl must conform to a uniform size of waist, this varying from eighteen to twenty inches, but never above twenty. Tall or short, fat or lean, Nature must stand aside, and the hour-glass serve as model, the results simply adding one more factor of destruction to the number already ranged against the girl.

The matter of regular meals has also far less attention than is necessary. Dinner is a "movable feast." The girls are allowed to go out only two or three at once, and often it is three o'clock or even later before some have broken the fast. Though there is often ample room for tea and coffee urns, the suggestion seems to be regarded as a dangerous innovation, holding under the innocent seeming, a possible social revolution. The thing that hath been shall be, and the obstinate hide-bound conservatism of the English shop-keeper is beyond belief till experience has made it certain. A few employers consider this matter. The majority ignore it as beneath consideration.

The question of suitable floor managers is really the comprehensive one, including almost every evil and every good that can come to the shop girl, whether in the East or West End. Here, as with us, the girl is absolutely in his power. He governs the whole system of fines, one uncomfortable but necessary feature of any large establishment, and injustice in these can have fullest possible play.

"The fines are an awful nuisance, that they are," said a bright-faced girl in one of the best-known shops of London—a great bazar, much like Macy's. "But then it all depends on the manager. Some of them are real nasty, you know, and if they happen not to like a girl, they stick on fines just to spite her. You see we're in their power, and some of them just love to show it and bully the girls no end. And worse than that, they're impudent too if a girl is pretty, and often she doesn't dare complain, for fear of losing the place, and he has it all his own way. This department's got a very fair manager, and we all like him. He's careful about fines, and plans about our dinners and all that, so we're better off than most. The manager does what he pleases everywhere."

These facts are for the West End, where dealings are nominally fair, and where wages may, in some exceptional case, run as high as eighteen shillings or even a pound a week. But the average falls far below this, from ten to fourteen being the usual figures, while seven and eight may be the sum. This, for the girl who lives at home, represents dress and pocket-money, but the great majority must support themselves entirely. We have already seen what this sum can do for the shirt-maker and general needlewoman, and it is easy to judge how the girl fares for whom the weekly wage is less. In the East End it falls sometimes as low as three shillings and sixpence (84c.). The girls club together, huddling in small back rooms, and spending all that can be saved on dress. Naturally, unless with exceptionally keen consciences, they find what is called "sin" an easier fact than starvation; and so the story goes on, and out of greed is born the misery, which, at last, compels greed to heavier poor rates, and thus an approximation to the distribution of the profit which should have been the worker's.

Here, as in all cities, the place seems to beckon every girl ambitious of something beyond domestic service. There are cheap amusements, "penny-gaffs" and the like, the "penny-gaff" being the equivalent of our dime museum. There is the companionship of the fellow-worker; the late going home through brightly-lighted streets, and the crowding throng of people,—all that makes the alleviation of the East End life; and there is, too, the chance, always possible, of a lover and a husband, perhaps a grade above, or many grades above, their beginning or their present lives. This alone is impulse and hope.

CHAPTER XII.

FROM COVENT GARDEN TO THE EEL-SOUP MAN IN THE BOROUGH.

Now and then, in the long search into the underlying causes of effects which are plain to all men's eyes, one pauses till the rush of impressions has ceased, and it is possible again to ignore this many-sided, demanding London, which makes a claim unknown to any other city of the earth save Rome. But there is a certain justification in lingering at points where women and children congregate, since their life also is part of the quest, and nowhere can it better be seen than in and about Covent Garden Market,—a thousand thoughts arising as the old square is entered from whatever point.

It is not alone the first days of the pilgrim's wanderings in London that are filled with the curious sense of home coming that makes up the consciousness of many an American. It is as if an old story were told again, and the heir, stolen in childhood, returned, unrecognized by those about him, but recalling with more and more freshness and certainty the scenes of which he was once a part. The years slip away. Two hundred and more of them lie between, it is true; but not two hundred nor ten times two hundred can blot out the lines of a record in which the struggle and the hope of all English-speaking people was one. For past or present alike, London stands as the fountain-head; and thus, whatever pain may come from the oppressive sense of crowded, swarming life pent up in these dull gray walls, whatever conviction that such a monster mass of human energy and human pain needs diffusion and not concentration, London holds and will hold a fascination that is quite apart from any outward aspect.

To go to a point determined upon beforehand is good. To lose oneself in the labyrinth of lanes and alleys and come suddenly upon something quite as desirable, is even better; and this losing is as inevitable as the finding also becomes. The first perplexity arises from the fact that a London street is "everything by turns and nothing long," and that a solitary block of buildings owns often a name as long as itself. The line of street which, on the map, appears continuous, gives a dozen changes to the mile, and the pilgrim discovers quickly that he is always somewhere else than at or on the point determined upon. Then the temptation to add to this complication by sudden excursions into shadowy courts and dark little passages is irresistible, not to mention the desire, equally pressing, of discovering at once if Violet Lane and Hop Vine Alley and Myrtle Court have really any relation to their names, or are simply the reaching out of their inhabitants for some touch of Nature's benefactions. Violet Lane may have had its hedgerows and violets in a day long dead, precisely as hop vines may have flung their pale green bells over cottage paling, for both are far outside the old city limits; but to-day they are simply the narrowest of passages between the grimiest of buildings, given over to trade in its most sordid form, with never a green leaf even to recall the country hedgerows long since only memory.

It is a matter of no surprise, then, to find that Covent Garden holds no hint of its past save in name, though from the noisy Strand one has passed into so many sheltered, quiet nooks unknown to nine tenths of the hurrying throng in that great artery of London, that one half expects to see the green trees and the box-bordered alleys of the old garden where the monks once walked. Far back in the very beginning of the thirteenth century it was the convent garden of Westminster, and its choice fruits and flowers rejoiced the soul of the growers, who planted and pruned with small thought of what the centuries were to bring. Through all chances and changes it remained a garden up to 1621, when much of the original ground had been swallowed up by royal grants, and one duke and another had built his town-house amid the spreading trees; for this "amorous and herbivorous parish," as Sidney Smith calls it, was one of the most fashionable quarters of London. The Stuart kings and their courts delighted in it, and the square was filled with houses designed by Inigo Jones, the north and east side of the market having an arcade called the "Portico Walk," but soon changed to the name which it has long borne,—the "Piazza." The market went on behind these pillars, but year by year, as London grew, pushed itself toward the centre of the square, till now not a foot of vacant space remains. At one of its stalls may still be found an ancient marketman, whose name, Anthony Piazza, is a memory of a parish custom which named after this favorite walk many of the foundling children born in the parish.

There is nothing more curious in all London than the transformations known to this once quiet spot. Drury Lane is close at hand, and Covent Garden Theatre is as well known as the market itself. The convent has become a play-house. "Monks and nuns turn actors and actresses. The garden, formal and quiet, where a salad was cut for a lady abbess, and flowers were gathered to adorn images, becomes a market, noisy and full of life, distributing its thousands of fruits and flowers to a vicious metropolis." Two quaint old inns are still here; two great national theatres, and a churchyard full of mouldy but still famous celebrities,—the church itself, bare and big, rising above them. In the days of the Stuarts, people prayed to be buried here hardly less than in Westminster Abbey, and the lover of epitaph and monument will find occupation for many an hour. This strange, squat old building, under the shadow of the church, is the market, its hundred columns and chapel-looking fronts always knee-deep and more in baskets and fruits and vegetables, while its air still seems to breathe of old books, old painters, and old authors.

"Night and morning are at meeting," for Covent Garden makes small distinction between the two, and whether it is a late supper or an early breakfast that the coffee-rooms and stalls are furnishing, can hardly be determined by one who has elected to know how the market receives and how it distributes its supplies. In November fog and mist, or the blackness of early winter, with snow on the ground, or cold rain falling, resolution is needed for such an expedition, and still more, if one would see all that the deep night hides, and that comes to light as the dawn struggles through. This business of feeding a city of four million people seems the simplest and most natural of occupations; but the facts involved are staggering, not alone in the mere matter of quantities and the amazement at the first sight of them, but in the thousands of lives tangled with them. Quantity is the first impression. Every cellar runs over with green stuff, mountains of which come in on enormous wagons and fill up all spaces left vacant, heaving masses of basket stumbling from other wagons and filling with instant celerity. In the great vans pour, from every market garden and outlying district of London, from all England, from the United Kingdom, from all the world, literally; for it is soon discovered that these enormous vehicles on high springs and with immense wheels, drawn by Normandy horses of size and strength to match, are chiefly from the railway stations, and that the drivers, who seem to be built on the same plan as the horses and vans, have big limbs and big voices and a high color, and that the bulging pockets of their velveteen suits show invoices and receipt books.

Not alone from railway stations and trains, from which tons of cabbages, carrots, onions, and all the vegetable tribe issue, but from the docks where steamers from Rotterdam and Antwerp and India and America, and all that lie between, come the contributions, ranged presently in due order in stall and arcade. There is no hint of anything grosser than the great cabbages, which appear to be London's favorite vegetable. Meat has its place at Smithfield, and fish at Billingsgate, but the old garden is, in one sense, true to its name, and gives us only the kindly fruits of the earth, with their transformations into butter and cheese.

In the central arcade fruit has the honors, and no prettier picture can well be imagined. For once under these gray skies there is a sense of color and light, and there is no surprise in hearing that Turner came here to study both, and that even the artist of to-day does not disdain the same method.

It is the flower-market, however, to which one turns with a certainty gained at once that no disappointment follows intimate acquaintance with English flowers. There are exotics for those who will, but it is not with them that one lingers. It is to the hundreds upon hundreds of flower-pots, in which grow roses and geraniums and mignonette and a score with old-fashioned but forever beloved names. There are great bunches of mignonette for a penny, and lesser bunches of sweet odors for the same coin, while the violets have rows of baskets to themselves, as indeed they need, for scores of buyers flock about them,—little buyers chiefly, with tangled hair and bare feet and the purchase-money tied in some corner of their rags; for they buy to sell again, and having tramped miles it may be to this fountain-head, will tramp other miles before night comes, making their way into court and alley and under sunless doorways, crying "Violets! sweet violets!" as they were cried in Herrick's time. A ha'penny will buy one of the tiny bunches which they have made up with swift fingers, and they are bought even by the poorest; how, heaven only knows. But, in cracked jug or battered tin, the bunch of violets sweetens the foul air, or the bit of mignonette grows and even thrives, where human kind cannot.

So, though Covent Garden has in winter "flowers at guineas apiece, pineapples at guineas a pound, and peas at guineas a quart,"—these for the rich only,—it has also its possibilities for the poor. They throng about it at all times, for there is always a chance of some stray orange or apple or rejected vegetable that will help out a meal. They throng above all in these terrible days when the "unemployed" are huddling under arches and in dark places where they lay their homeless heads, and where, in the hours between night and morning, the cocoa-rooms open for the hungry drivers of the big vans, who pour down great mugs of coffee and cocoa, and make away with mountains of bread and butter. A penny gives a small mug of cocoa and a slice of bread and butter, and the owner of a penny is rich. Often it is shared, and the sharer, half drunk still, it may be, and foul with the mud and refuse into which he crawled, can hardly be known as human, save for this one gleam of something beyond the human. Gaunt forms barely covered with rags, hollow eyes fierce with hunger, meet one at every turn in this early morning; and for many there is not even the penny, and they wait, sometimes with appeal, but as often silently, the chance gift of the buyer. Food for all the world, it would seem, and yet London is not fed; and having once looked upon these waifs that are floated against the pillars of the old market, one fancies almost a curse on the piles of food that is not for them save as charity gives it, and the flowers that even on graves will never be theirs.

Men and women huddle here, and under the arches, children skulk away like young rats, feeding on offal, lying close in dark corners for warmth, and hunted about also like rats. It is a poverty desperate and horrible beyond that that any other civilized city can show; and who shall say who is responsible, or what the end will be?

So the question lingers with one, as the market is left, and one passes on and out to the Strand and its motley stream of life, lingering through Fleet Street and the winding ways into the City, past St. Paul's, and still on till London Bridge is reached and the Borough is near. Fare as one may, north or south, west or east, there is no escape from the sullen roar of the great city, a roar like the beat of a stormy sea against cliffs. An hour and more ago, that perplexed and baffled luminary the sun has struggled up through strange shapes and hues of morning cloud, and for a few minutes asserted his right to rule. But the gleam of gold and crimson brought with him has given way to the grays and black which make up chiefly what the Londoners call sky, and over London Bridge one passes on into the dim grayness merging into something darker and more cheerless. On the Borough Road there should be some escape,—that Borough Road on which the Canterbury Pilgrims rode out on a morning less complicated, it is certain, by fog and mist and smoke and soot than mornings that dawn for this generation. Every foot of the way is history; the old Tower at one's back, and the past as alive as the present. "Merrie England" was at its best, they say, when the pages we know were making; but here as elsewhere, the name is a tradition, belied by every fact of the present.

The old inns along the way still hold their promise of good cheer, and the great kitchens and tap-rooms have seen wild revelry enough; but even for them has been the sight of political or other martyr done to death in their court-yards, while no foot of playground, no matter how much the people's own, but has been steeped in blood and watered with tears of English matron and maid. If "Merrie England" deserved its name, it must have come from a determination as fixed as Mark Tapley's, to be jolly under any and all circumstances, and certainly circumstances have done their best to favor such resolution. The peasant of the past, usually represented as dancing heavily about a Maypole, or gazing contentedly at some procession of his lords and masters as it swept by, has no counterpart to-day, nor will his like come again. For here about the old Borough, where every stone means history and the "making of the English people," there are faces of all types that England holds, but no face yet seen carries any sense of merriment, or any good thing that might bear its name. It is the burden of living that looks from dull eyes and stolid faces, and a hopelessness, unconscious it may be but always apparent, that better things may come. The typical Englishman, as we know him, has but occasional place, and the mass, hurrying to and fro in the midst of this roar of traffic, are thin and eager and restless of countenance as any crowd of Americans in the same type of surroundings. Innumerable little streets, each dingier and more sordid than the last, open on either side. Hot coffee and cocoa cans are at every corner, their shining brass presided over by men chiefly. Here, as throughout East London, sellers of every sort of eatable and drinkable thing wander up and down.

Paris is credited with living most of its life under all men's eyes, and London certainly may share this reputation as far as eating goes. In fact, working London, taking the poorest class both in pay and rank, has small space at home for much cookery, and finds more satisfaction in the flavor of food prepared outside. The throats, tanned and parched by much beer, are sensitive only to something with the most distinct and defined taste of its own; and so it is that whelks and winkles and mussels and all forms of fish and flesh, that are to the American uneatably strong and unpleasant, make the luxuries of the English poor. They are conservative, also, like all the poor, and prefer old acquaintances to new; and the costers and sellers of all sorts realize this, and seldom go beyond an established list.

It is always "somethin' 'ot" that the workman craves; and small wonder, when one has once tested London climate, and found that, nine months out of twelve, fog and mist creep chill into bones and marrow, and that a fire is comfortable even in July. November accents this fact sharply, and by November the pea-soup and eel-soup men are at their posts, and about market and dock, and in lane and alley, the trade is brisk. Near Petticoat Lane, one of the oddest of London's odd corners, small newsboys rush up and take a cupful as critically as I have seen them take waffles from the old women purveyors of these delicacies about City Hall Park and Park Row, while hungry costers and workmen appear to find it the most satisfactory of meals.

One must have watched the eel baskets at Billingsgate, and then read the annual consumption, before it is possible to understand how street after street has its eel-pie house, and how the stacks of small pies in the windows are always disappearing and always being renewed. It would seem with eel pies as with oysters, of which Sam Weller stated his conviction that the surprising number of shops and stalls came from the fact that the moment a man found himself in difficulties he "rushed out and ate oysters in reg'lar desperation." It is certain that some of the eaters look desperate enough; but the seller is a middle-aged, quiet-looking man, who eyes his customers sharply, but serves them with generous cupfuls. The sharpness is evidently acquired, and not native, and he has need of it, the London newsboys, who are his best patrons, being ready to drive a bargain as keen as their fellows on the other side of the sea. His stand is opposite a cat's-meat market, a sausage shop in significant proximity, and he endures much chaffing as to the make-up of his pea soup, which he sells in its season. But it is eels for which the demand is heaviest and always certain, and the eel-soup man's day begins early and ends late, on Saturdays lasting well into Sunday morning. He is prosperous as such business goes, and buys four "draughts" of eels on a Friday for the Saturday's work, a "draught" being twenty pounds, while now and then he has been known to get rid of a hundred pounds.

This stall, to which the newsboys flock as being more "stylish" than most of its kind, is fitted with a cast-iron fireplace holding two large kettles of four or five gallon capacity. A dozen pint bowls, or basins as the Englishman prefers to call them, and an equal number of half-pint cups, with spoons for all, constitute the outfit; and even for the poorest establishment of the sort, a capital of not less than a pound is required. This stall has four lamps with "Hot Eels" painted on them, and one side of it is given to whelks, which are boiled at home and always eaten cold with abundance of vinegar, of which the newsboy is prodigal. At times fried fish are added to the stock, but eels lead, and mean the largest profit on the amount invested.

Dutch eels are preferred, and the large buyer likes to go directly to the eel boats at the Billingsgate Wharf and buy the squirming draughts, fresh from the tanks in which they have been brought. To dress and prepare a draught takes about three hours, and the daughter of the stall-owner stands at one side engaged in this operation, cleaning, washing, and cutting up the eels into small pieces from half an inch to an inch long. These are boiled, the liquor being made smooth and thick with flour, and flavored with chopped parsley and mixed spices, principally allspice. For half a penny, from five to seven pieces may be had, the cup being then filled up with the liquor, to which the buyer is allowed to add vinegar at discretion. There is a tradition of one customer so partial to hot eels that he used to come twice a day and take eight cupfuls a day, four at noon and four as a night-cap.

The hot-eel season ends with early autumn, and pea soup takes its place, though a small proportion of eels is always to be had. Split peas, celery, and beef bones are needed for this, and it is here that the cat's-meat man is supposed to be an active partner. In any case the smell is savory, and the hot steam a constant invitation to the shivering passers-by. This man has no cry of "Hot Eels!" like many of the sellers.

"I touches up people's noses; 't ain't their heyes or their hears I'm hafter," he says, though the neat stall makes its own claim on the "heyes."

In another alley is another pea-soup man, one-legged, but not at all depressed by this or any other circumstance of fate. He makes, or his wife makes, the pea soup at home, and he keeps it hot by means of a charcoal fire in two old tin saucepans.

"Hard work?" he says. "You wouldn't think so if you'd been on your back seven months and four days in Middlesex Orspital. I was a coal heaver, and going along easy and natural over the plank from one barge to another, and there come the swell from some steamers and threw up the plank and chucked me off, and I broke my knee against the barge. It's bad now. I'd ought to 'ad it hoff, an' so the surgeons said; but I wouldn't, an' me wife wouldn't, and the bone keeps workin' out, and I've 'ad nineteen months all told in the 'orspital, and Lord knows how me wife and the young uns got on. I was bad enough off, I was, till a neighbor o' mine, a master butcher, told me there was a man up in Clare Market, makin' a fortune at hot eels and pea soup, and he lent me ten shillings to start in that line. He and me wife's the best friends I've ever had in the world; for I've no memory of a mother, and me father died at sea. My oldest daughter, she's a good un, goes for the eels and cuts 'em up, and she an' me wife does all the hard work. I've only to sit at the stall and sell, and they do make 'em tasty. There's no better. But we're hard up. I'd do better if I'd a little more money to buy with. I can't get a draught like some of the men, and them that gets by the quantity can give more. The boys tells me there's one man gives 'em as much as eight pieces; that's what they calls a lumping ha'p'worth. And the liquor's richer when you boils up so many eels. What's my tin pot ag'in' his five-gallon one? There's even some that boils the 'eads, and sells 'em for a farthing a cupful; but I've not come to that. But we're badly off. The missus has a pair o' shoes, and she offs with 'em when my daughter goes to market, and my boy the youngest 's got no shoes; but we do very well, and would do better, only the cheap pie shop takes off a lot o' trade. I wouldn't eat them pies. It's the dead eels that goes into 'em, and we that handles eels knows well enough that they're rank poison if they ain't cut up alive, and the flesh of 'em squirming still when they goes into the boiling water. Them pies is uncertain, anyway, whatever kind you buy. I've seen a man get off a lot a week old, just with the dodge of hot spiced gravy poured out of an oil can into a hole in the lid, and that gravy no more'n a little brown flour and water; but the spice did it. The cat's-meat men knows; oh, yes! they knows what becomes of what's left when Saturday night comes, though I've naught to say ag'in' the cat's-meat men, for it's a respectable business enough.

"I've thought of other ways. There's the baked-potato men, but the 'ansome can and fixin's for keeping 'em 'ot is what costs, you see. Trotters is profitable, too, if you've a start, that is, though it's women mostly that 'andles trotters, blest if I know why! I've a cousin in the boiled pudding business—meat puddings and fruit, too;—but it's all going out, along of the bakers that don't give poor folks a chance. They has their big coppers, and boils up their puddings by the 'undred; but I dare say there's no more need o' street-sellers, for folks go to shops for most things now. She's in Leather Lane, this cousin o' mine, and makes plum-duff as isn't to be beat; but she sells Saturday nights mostly, and for Sunday dinners. Ginger nuts goes off well, but there again the shops 'as you, and unless you can make a great show, with brass things shining to put your eyes out, and a stall that looks as well as a shop, you're nowhere. There's no chance for the poor anyhow, it seems to me; for even if you get a start, there's always some one with more money to do the thing better, and so take the bread out of your mouth. But 'better' 's only more show often, and me wife can't be beat for tastiness, whether it's hot eels or pea soup, and I'll say that long as I stand."

So many small trades have been ruined by the larger shops taking them up, that the street-seller's case becomes daily a more complicated one, and the making a living by old-fashioned and time-honored methods almost impossible. It is all part of the general problem of the day, and the street-sellers, whether costers or those of lower degree, look forward apprehensively to changes which seem on the way, and puzzle their untaught minds as to why each avenue of livelihood seems more and more barred against them. For the poorest there seems only a helpless, dumb acquiescence in the order of things which they are powerless to change; but the looker-on, who watches the mass of misery crowding London streets or hiding away in attic and cellar, knows that out of such conditions sudden fury and revolt is born, and that, if the prosperous will not heed and help while they may, the time comes when help will be with no choice of theirs.

CHAPTER XIII.

WOMEN IN GENERAL TRADES.

As investigation progresses, it becomes at times a question as to which of two great factors must dominate the present status of women as workers; competition, which blinds the eyes to anything but the surest way of obtaining the proper per cent, or the inherited Anglo-Saxon brutality, which, in its lowest form of manifestation, makes the English wife-beater. It is certain that the English workingwoman has not only the disabilities which her American sister also faces,—some inherent in herself, and as many arising from the press of the present system,—but added to this the apparent incapacity of the employer to see that they have rights of any description whatsoever. Even the factory act and the various attempts to legislate in behalf of women and child workers strikes the average employer as a gross interference with his constitutional rights. Where he can he evades. Where he cannot he is apt to grow purple over the impertinence of meddling reformers who cannot let well-enough alone.

Such a representative of one class of English employers is to be found in a little street, not a stone's throw from Fleet Street, the great newspaper centre, where all day long one meets authors, editors, and journalists of every degree. Toward eight in the morning, as at the same hour in the evening, another crowd is to be seen, made up of hundreds upon hundreds of girls hurrying to the countless printing establishments of every grade, which are to be found in every street and court opening from or near Fleet Street. It is not newspaper interests alone that are represented there. The Temple, Inner, Outer, and Middle, with the magnificent group of buildings, also a part of the Temple's workings—the new courts of law, have each and all their quota of law printing, and a throng made up of every order of ability, from the reader of Greek proof down to the folder of Mother Siegel's Almanac, hurries through Fleet Street to the day's work.

In a building devoted to the printing and sending out of a popular weekly of the cheaper order, the lower rooms met all requisitions as to space and proper ventilation.

"We have nothing to hide," said the manager, "nothing at all. You may go from top to bottom if you will."

This was said at what appeared to be the end of an hour or two of going from room to room, watching the girls at work at the multitudinous phases involved, and wondering how energy enough remained after twelve hours of it, for getting home.

A flight of dark little stairs led up to a region even darker, and he changed color as we turned toward them.

"This is all temporary," he said hastily. "We are very much crowded for space, and we are going to move soon. We do the best we can in the mean time. It's only temporary."

This was the reason for the darkness. Stumbling up the open stairs, hardly more than a ladder, one came into a half story added to the original building, and so low that the manager bowed his head as he entered; nor was there any point at which he could stand freely upright, this well-fed Englishman nearly six feet tall. For the girls there was no such difficulty, and nearly two hundred were packed into the space, in which folding and stitching machines ran by steam, while at long tables other branches of the same work were going on by hand. The noise and the heat from gas-jets, steam, and the crowd of workers made the place hideous. The girls themselves appeared in no worse condition than many others seen that day, but were all alike, pale and anemic. Their hours were from 8 A. M. to 8 P. M., with an hour for dinner, usually from one to two. The law also allows half an hour for tea, but in all cases investigated, this time is docked if the girl takes it. Cheap "cocoa rooms" are all about, where a cup of tea or cocoa and a bun may be had for twopence; but even this is a heavy item to a girl who earns never more than ten shillings ($2.50) a week, and as often from four to seven or eight. No arrangement for making tea on the premises was to be found here or anywhere.

"We mean to have a room," the employers said, "but we have so many expenses attendant on the growing business that there doesn't seem any chance yet."

This employer brought his wage-book forward and showed with pride that several of his girls earned a pound a week ($5.00). But on turning back some pages, the record showed only fourteen and sixteen shillings for these same names, and after a pause the manager admitted that the pound had been earned by adding night work.

This question of whether night work is ever done had been a most difficult one to determine. The girls themselves declared that it often was, and that they liked it because they got three shillings and their breakfast; but the managers had in more than one case denied the charge with fury.

"It's over-work," the present one said, his eyes on the rows of figures.

"When?" asked my companion quietly, and he burst into a laugh.

"You've got me this time," he said. "You've given your word not to mention names, so I don't mind telling you. It's like this. There's a new firm to be floated, and they want two hundred thousand circulars on two days' notice. Of course it has to be night-work, and we put it through, but we give the girls time for supper, and provide a good breakfast, and there's hundreds waiting for the chance. But you've seen for yourselves. Some of them make a pound a week. What in reason does a woman want of more than a pound a week?"

This remark is the stereotyped one of quite two-thirds the employers, whether men or women. The old delusion still holds that a man works for others, a woman solely for herself, and although each woman should appear with those dependent upon her in entire or partial degree arranged in line, it would make no difference in the conviction. It is quite true that many married women work for pocket-money, and having homes, can afford to underbid legitimate workers. But they are the smallest proportion of this vast army of London toilers, whose pitiful wage is earned by a day's labor which happily has no counterpart in length with us, save among the lowest grade of needlewomen.

In the case under present consideration pay for over-time was allowed at the rate of fourpence an hour and a penny extra. If late five minutes the workwoman is fined twopence, and if not there by nine is "drilled," that is, sent away, or kept waiting near until two, when she goes on for half a day.

If tardy, as must often happen with fogs and other causes, she is often "drilled" for a week, though "drilling" in this trade is used more often with men than with women, who are less liable to irregularities caused by drink. In some establishments the bait of sixpence a week for good conduct is offered, but this is deducted on the faintest pretext, and the worker fined as well, for any violation of regulations tacit or written.

In another establishment piece-work alone was done, a popular almanac being folded at fourpence a thousand sheets. Railway tickets brought in from eight to ten shillings a week, and prize packages of stationery, fourpence a score, the folding and packing of prize doubling the length of time required and thus lessening wages in the same ratio.

I have given phases of this one trade in detail, because the same general rules govern all. The confectionery workers' wages are at about the same rate, although a pound a week is almost unknown, the girls making from three shillings and sixpence (84c.) to fourteen and sixteen shillings weekly. A large "butter-scotch" factory pays these rates and allows the weekly good-conduct sixpence which, however, few succeed in earning. This factory is managed by two brothers who take alternate weeks, and the younger one exacts from the girls an hour more a day than the older one. Here the factory act applies, and inspectors appear periodically; but this does not hinder the carrying out of individual theories as to what constitutes a day. If five minutes late, sevenpence is deducted from the week's wages, which begin at three and sixpence and ascend to nine, the latter price being the utmost to be earned in this branch of the trade.

In the cocoa rooms which are to be found everywhere in London where business of any sort is carried on, the pay ranges from ten to twelve shillings a week. The work is hard and incessant, although hours are often shorter. In both confectionery factories and the majority of factory trades, an hour is allowed for dinner, but the tea half hour refused or deducted from time. London in this respect, and indeed in most points affecting the comfort and well-being of operatives of every class, is far behind countries, the great manufacturing cities of which are doing much to lighten oppressive conditions and give some possibility of relaxation and improvement. Some of the best reforms in a factory life have begun in England, and it is thus all the more puzzling to find that indifference, often to a brutal degree, characterizes the attitude of many London employers, who have reduced wages to the lowest, and brought profits to the highest, attainable point. It is true that he is driven by a force often quite beyond his control, foreign competition, French and German, being no less sharp than that on his own soil. He must study chances of profit to a farthing, and in such study there is naturally small thought of his workers, save as hands in which the farthings may be found. Many a woman goes to her place of work, leaving behind her children who have breakfasted with her on "kettle broth," and will be happy if the same is certain at supper time.

"There's six of us have had nought but kettle broth for a fortnight," said one. "You know what that is? It's half a quarter loaf, soaked in hot water with a hap'orth of dripping and a spoonful of salt. When you've lived on that night and morning for a week or two, you can't help but long for a change, though, God forgive me! there's them that fares worse. But it'll be the broth without the bread before we're through. There's no living to be had in old England any more, and yet the rich folks don't want less. Do you know how it is, ma'am? Is there any chance of better times, do you think? Is it that they *want* us to starve? I've heard that said, but somehow it seems as if there must be hearts still, and they'll see soon, and then things'll be different. Oh, yes, they must be different."

Will they be different? It is unskilled workers who have just spoken, but do the skilled fare much better? I append a portion of a table of earnings, prepared a year or two since by the chaplain of the Clerkenwell prison, a thoughtful and earnest worker among the poor, this table ranking as one of the best of the attempts to discover the actual position of the workingwoman at present:—

"Making paper bags, 4½d. to 5½d. per thousand; possible earnings, 5s. to 9s. a week. Button-holes, 3d. per dozen; possible earnings, 8s. per week.

"Shirts 2d. each, worker finding her own cotton; can get six done between 6 A. M. and 11 P. M.

"Sack-sewing, 6d. for twenty-five, 8d. to 1s. 6d. per hundred; possible earnings, 7s. per week.

"Pill-box making, 1s. for thirty-six gross; possible earnings, 1s. 3d. a day.

"Button-hole making, 1d. per dozen; can do three or four dozen between 5 A. M. and dark.

"Whip-making, 1s. per dozen; can do a dozen per day.

"Trousers-finishing, 3d. to 5d. each, finding own cotton; can do four per day.

"Shirt-finishing, 3d. to 4d. per dozen."

So the list runs on through all the trades open to women. A pound a week is a fortune; half or a third of that amount the wages of two-thirds the women who earn in working London; nor are there indications that the scale will rise or that better days are in store for one of these toilers, patient, heavy-eyed, well-nigh hopeless of any good to come, and yet saying among themselves the words already given:—

"There must be hearts still, and they'll see soon, and then things'll be different. Oh, yes, they must be different."

CHAPTER XIV.

FRENCH AND ENGLISH WORKERS.

It is but a narrow streak of silver main that separates the two countries, whose story has been that of constant mutual distrust, varied by intervals of armed truce, in which each nation elected to believe that it understood the other. Not only the nation as a whole, however, but the worker in each, is far from any such possibility; and the methods of one are likely to remain, for a long time to come, a source of bewilderment to the other. That conditions on both sides of the Channel are in many points at their worst, and that the labor problem is still unsolved for both England and the Continent, remains a truth, though it is at once evident to the student of this problem that France has solved one or two phases of the equation over which England is still quite helpless.

There is a famous chapter in the history of Ireland, entitled "Snakes in Ireland," the contents of which are as follows:—

"There are no snakes in Ireland."

On the same principle it becomes at once necessary in writing on the slums of Paris, to arrange the summary of the situation: "There are no slums in Paris."

In the English sense there certainly are none; and for the difference in visible conditions, several causes are responsible. The searcher for such regions discovers before the first day ends that there are none practically; and though now and then, as all byways are visited, one finds remnants of old Paris, and a court or narrow lane in which crime might lurk or poverty hide itself, as a whole there is hardly a spot where sunshine cannot come, and the hideous squalor of London is absolutely unknown. One quarter alone is to be excepted in this statement, and with that we are to deal farther on. The seamstress in a London garret or the shop-worker in the narrow rooms of the East End lives in a gloom for which there is neither outward nor inward alleviation. Soot is king of the great city, and his prime ministers, Smoke and Fog, work together to darken every haunt of man, and to shut out every glimpse of sun or moon. The flying flakes are in the air. Every breath draws them in; every moment leaves its deposit on wall and floor and person. The neatest and most determined fighter of dirt must still be bond slave to its power; and eating and drinking and breathing soot all day and every day, there comes at last an acquiescence in the consequences, and only an instinctive battle with the outward effects.

For the average worker, at the needle at least, wages are too low to admit of much soap; hot water is equally a luxury, and time if taken means just so much less of the scanty pay; and thus it happens that London poverty takes on a hopelessly grimy character, and that the visitor in the house of the workers learns to wear a uniform which shows as little as possible of the results of rising up and sitting down in the soot, which, if less evident in the home of the millionnaire, works its will no less surely.

Fresh from such experience, and with the memory of home and work room, manufactory or great shop, all alike sombre and depressing, the cleanliness of Paris, enforced by countless municipal regulations, is at first a constant surprise. The French workwoman, even of the lowest order, shares in the national characteristic which demands a fair exterior whatever may be the interior condition, and she shares also in the thrift which is equally a national possession, and the exercise of which has freed France from the largest portion of her enormous debt. The English workwoman of the lowest order, the trouser-stitcher or bag-maker, is not only worn and haggard to the eye, but wears a uniform of ancient bonnet and shawl, both of which represent the extremity of dejection. She clings to this bonnet as the type and suggestion of respectability and to the shawl no less; but the first has reached a point wherein it is not only grotesque but pitiful, the remnants of flowers and ribbons and any shadowy hint of ornamentation having long ago yielded to weather and age and other agents of destruction. The shawl or cloak is no less abject and forlorn, both being the badge of a condition from which emergence has become practically impossible. These lank figures carry no charm of womanhood,—nothing that can draw from sweater or general employer more than a sneer at the quality of the labor of those waiting always in numbers far beyond any real demand, until for both the adjective comes to be "superfluous," and employer and employed alike wonder why the earth holds them, and what good there is in an existence made up simply of want and struggle.

Precisely the opposite condition holds for the French worker, who, in the midst of problems as grave, faces them with the light-heartedness of her nation. She has learned to the minutest fraction what can be extracted from every centime, and though she too must shiver with cold, and go half-fed and half-clothed, every to-morrow holds the promise of something better, and to-day is thus made more bearable. She shares too the conviction, which has come to be part of the general faith concerning Paris, which seems always an embodied assurance, that sadness and want are impossible. Even her beggars, a good proportion of them laboriously made up for the parts they are to fill, find repression of cheerfulness their most difficult task, and smile confidingly on the sceptical observer of their methods, as if to make him a partner in the encouraging and satisfactory nature of things in general. The little seamstress who descends from her attic for the bread with its possible salad or bit of cheese which will form her day's ration, smiles also as she pauses to feel the thrill of life in the thronging boulevards and beautiful avenues, the long sweeps of which have wiped out for Paris as a whole everything that could by any chance be called slum.

Even in the narrowest street this stir of eager life penetrates, and every Parisian shares it and counts it as a necessity of daily existence. If shoes are too great a luxury, the workwoman clatters along in *sabots*, congratulating herself that they are cheap and that they never wear out. Custom, long-established and imperative, orders that she shall wear no head-covering, and thus she escapes the revelation bound up in the London worker's bonnet. Inherited instinct and training from birth have taught her hands the utmost skill with the needle. She makes her own dress, and wears it with an air which may in time transfer itself to something choicer; and this quality is in no whit affected by the the cheapness of the material. It may be only a print or some woollen stuff of the poorest order; but it and every detail of her dress represent something to which the English woman has not attained, and which temperament and every fact of life will hinder her attaining.

As I write, the charcoal-woman has climbed the long flights to the fifth floor, bending under the burden of an enormous sack of *charbon à terre*, but smiling as she puts it down. She is mistress of a little shop just round the corner, and she keeps the accounts of the wood and coal bought by her patrons by a system best known to herself, her earnings hardly going beyond three francs a day. Even she, black with the coal-dust which she wastes no time in scrubbing off save on Sundays when she too makes one of the throng in the boulevards, faces the hard labor with light-hearted confidence, and plans to save a sou here and there for the *dot* of the baby who shares in the distribution of coal-dust, and will presently trot by her side as assistant.

In the laundry just beyond, the women are singing or chattering, the voices rising in that sudden fury of words which comes upon this people, and makes the foreigner certain that bloodshed is near, but which ebbs instantly and peacefully, to rise again on due occasion. Long hours, exhausting labor, small wages, make no difference. The best worker counts from three to four francs daily as prosperity, and the rate has even fallen below this; yet they make no complaint, quite content with the sense of companionship, and with the satisfaction of making each article as perfect a specimen of skill as can be produced.

Here lies a difference deeper than that of temperament,—the fact that the French worker finds pleasure in the work itself, and counts its satisfactory appearance as a portion of the reward. Slop work, with its demand for speedy turning out of as many specimens of the poorest order per day as the hours will allow, is repugnant to every instinct of the French workwoman; and thus it happens that even slop work on this side of the Channel holds some hint of ornamentation and the desire to lift it out of the depth to which it has fallen. But it is gaining ground, fierce competition producing this effect everywhere; and the always lessening ratio of wages which attends its production, must in time bring about the same disastrous results here as elsewhere, unless the tide is arrested, and some form of co-operative production takes its place. With the French worker in the higher forms of needle industry we shall deal in the next chapter, finding what differences are to be met here also between French and English methods.

CHAPTER XV.

FRENCH BARGAIN COUNTERS.

"Yes, it is the great shops that have done that, madame. Once, you saw what was only well finished and a credit to the worker, and, even if the reward was small, she had pride in the work and her own skill, and did always her best. But now, what will you? The thing must be cheap, cheapest. The machine to sew hurries everything, and you find the workwoman sans ambition and busy only to hurry and be one with the machine. It is wrong, all wrong, but that is progress, and one must submit. When the small shops had place to live, and the great *magasins* were not for ladies or any who wished the best, then it was different, but now all is changed, and work has no character. It is all the same; always the machine."

More than once this plaint has been made, and the sewing-machine accused as the cause of depression in wages, of deterioration of all hand needlework, and of the originality that once distinguished French productions; and there is some truth in the charge, not only for Paris, but for all cities to which needlewomen throng. Machinery has gradually revolutionized all feminine industries in Paris, and its effect is not only on the general system of wages, but upon the moral condition of the worker, and family life as a whole has become to the student of social questions one of gravest importance. On the one hand is the conviction, already quoted, that it has brought with it deterioration in every phase of the work; on the other, that it is an educating and beneficent agent, raising the general standard of wages, and putting three garments where once but one could be owned. It is an old story, and will give food for speculation in the future, quite as much as in the past. But in talking with skilled workers, from dressmakers to the needlewomen employed on trousseaux and the most delicate forms of this industry, each has expressed the same conviction, and this quite apart from the political economist's view that there must be a return to hand production, if the standard is not to remain hopelessly below its old place. Such return would not necessarily exclude machinery, which must be regarded as an indispensable adjunct to the worker's life. It would simply put it in its proper place,—that of aid, but never master. It is the spirit of competition which is motive power to-day, and which drives the whirring wheels and crowds the counters of every shop with productions which have no merit but that of cheapness, and the price of which means no return to the worker beyond the barest subsistence.

Subsistence in Paris has come to mean something far different from the facts of a generation ago. Wages have always been fixed at a standard barely above subsistence; but, even under these conditions, French frugality has succeeded not only in living, but in putting by a trifle month by month. As the great manufactories have sprung up, possibilities have lessened and altered, till the workwoman, however cheerfully she may face conditions, knows that saving has become impossible. If, in some cases, wages have risen, prices have advanced with them till only necessities are possible, the useful having dropped away from the plan, and the agreeable ceased to have place even in thought. Even before the long siege, and the semi-starvation that came to all within the walls of Paris, prices had been rising, and no reduction has come which even approximates to the old figures. Every article of daily need is at the highest point, sugar alone being an illustration of what the determination to protect an industry has brought about. The London workwoman buys a pound for one penny, or at the most twopence. The French workwoman must give eleven or twelve sous, and then have only beet sugar, which has not much over half the saccharine quality of cane sugar. Flour, milk, eggs, all are equally high, meat alone being at nearly the same prices as in London. Fruit is a nearly impossible luxury, and fuel so dear that shivering is the law for all but the rich, while rents are also far beyond London prices, with no "improved dwellings" system to give the utmost for the scanty sum at disposal. For the needlewoman the food question has resolved itself into bread alone, for at least one meal, with a little coffee, chiefly chicory, and possibly some vegetable for the others. But many a one lives on bread for six days in the week, reserving the few sous that can be saved for a Sunday bit of meat, or bones for soup. Even the system which allows of buying "portions," just enough for a single individual, is valueless for her, since the smallest and poorest portion is far beyond the sum which can never be made to stretch far enough for such indulgence.

"I have tried it, madame," said the same speaker, who had mourned over the degeneration of finish among the workwomen. "It was the siege that compelled it in the beginning, and then there was no complaining, since it was the will of the good God for all. But there came a time when sickness had been with me long, and I found no work but to stitch in my little room far up under the roof, and all the long hours bringing so little,—never more than two and a half francs, and days when it was even less; and then I found how one must live. I was proud, and wished to tell no one; but there was an *ouvrière* next me, in a little room, even smaller than mine, and she saw well that she could help, and that together some things might be possible that were not alone. She had her furnace for the fire, and we used it together on the days when we could make our soup, or the coffee that I missed more than all,—more, even, than wine, which is for us the same as water to you. It was months that I went not beyond fifty centimes a day for food, save the Sundays, and then but little more, since one grows at last to care little, and a good meal for one day makes the next that is wanting harder, I think, than when one wants always. But I am glad that I know; so glad that I could even wish the same knowledge for many who say, 'Why do they not live on what they earn? Why do they not have thrift, and make ready for old age?' Old age comes fast, it is true. Such years as I have known are double, yes, and treble, and one knows that they have shortened life. But when I say now 'the poor,' I know what that word means, and have such compassion as never before. It is the workers who are the real poor, and for them there is little hope, since it is the system that must change. It is the middleman who makes the money, and there are so many of them, how can there be much left for the one who comes last, and is only the machine that works?

"All that is true of England, and I have had two years there, and thus know well; all that is true, too, here, though we know better how we can live, and not be always so *triste* and sombre. But each day, as I go by the great new shops that have killed all the little ones, and by the great factory where electricity makes the machines go, and the women too become machines,— each day I know that these counters, where one can buy for a song, are counters where flesh and blood are sold. For, madame, it is starvation for the one who has made these garments; and why must one woman starve that another may wear what her own hands could make if she would? Everywhere it is *occasions* [bargains] that the great shops advertise.

Everywhere they must be more and more, and so wages lessen, till there is no more hope of living; and, because they lessen, marriage waits, and all that the good God meant for us waits also."

On the surface it is all well. There is less incompetency among French than English workers, and thus the class who furnish them need less arraignment for their lack of thoroughness. They contend, also, with one form of competition, which has its counterpart in America among the farmers' wives, who take the work at less than regular rates. This form is the convent work, which piles the counters, and is one of the most formidable obstacles to better rates for the worker. Innumerable convents make the preparation of underwear one of their industries, and, in the classes of girls whom they train to the needle, find workers requiring no wages, the training being regarded as equivalent. Naturally, their prices can be far below the ordinary market one, and thus the worker, benefited on the one hand, is defrauded on the other. In short, the evil is a universal one,—an integral portion of the present manufacturing system,—and its abolition can come only from roused public sentiment, and combination among the workers themselves.

CHAPTER XVI.

THE CITY OF THE SUN.

It is only with weeks of experience that the searcher into the under world of Paris life comes to any sense of real conditions, or discovers in what directions to look for the misery which seldom floats to the surface, and which even wears the face of content. That there are no slums, and that acute suffering is in the nature of things impossible, is the first conviction, and it remains in degree even when both misery and its lurking-places have become familiar sights. Paris itself, gay, bright, beautiful, beloved of every dweller within its walls, so dominates that shadows seem impossible, and as one watches the eager throng in boulevard or avenue, or the laughing, chattering groups before even the poorest café, other life than this sinks out of sight. The most meagrely paid needlewoman, the most overworked toiler in trades, indoors or out, seizes any stray moment for rest or small pleasures, and from a half-franc bottle of wine, or some pretence of lemonade or sugar water, extracts entertainment for half a dozen. The pressure in actual fact remains the same. Always behind in the shadow lurks starvation, and there is one street, now very nearly wiped out, known to its inhabitants still as "*la rue où l'on ne meurt jamais*"—the street where one never dies, since every soul therein finds their last bed in the hospital. This is the *quartier* Mouffetard, where bits of old Paris are still discernible, and where strange trades are in operation; industries which only a people so pinched and driven by sharp necessity could ever have invented.

The descent to these is a gradual one, and most often the women who are found in them have known more than one occupation, and have been, in the beginning at least, needlewomen of greater or less degree of skill. Depression of wages, which now are at the lowest limit of subsistence, drives them into experiments in other directions, and often failing sight or utter weariness of the monotonous employment is another cause. These form but a small proportion of such workers, who generally are a species of guild, a family having begun some small new industry and gradually drawn in others, till a body of workers in the same line is formed, strong enough to withstand any interlopers.

"What becomes of the women who are too old to sew, and who have never gained skill enough to earn more than a bare living?" I asked one day of a seamstress whose own skill was unquestioned, but who, even with this in her favor, averages only three francs a day.

"They do many things, madame. One who is my neighbor is now scrubber and cleaner, and is happily friends with a '*concierge*,' who allows her to aid him. That is a difficulty for all who would do that work. It is that the '*concierges*,' whether men or women, think that any pay from the '*locataires*' must be for them; and so they will never tell the tenant of a woman who seeks work, but will say always, 'It is I who can do it all. One cannot trust these from the outside.' But for her, as I say, there is opportunity, and at last she has food, when as '*couturière*' it was quite—yes, quite impossible. There was a child, an idiot—the child of her daughter who is dead, and from whom she refuses always to be separated, and she sews always on the sewing-machine, till sickness comes, and it is sold for rent and many things. She is proud. She has not wished to scrub and clean, but for such work is twenty-five centimes an hour, and often food that the tenant does not wish. At times they give her less, and in any case one calculates always the time and watches very closely, but for her, at least, is more money than for many years; sometimes even three francs, if a day has been good. But that is but seldom, and she must carry her own soap and brush, and pay for all.

"That is one way, and there is another that fills me with terror, madame, lest I, too, may one day find myself in it. It is last and worst of all for women, I think. It is when they wear '*le cachemire d'osier*.' You do not know it, madame. It is the chiffonieress basket which she bears as a badge, and which she hangs at night, it may be, in the City of the Sun. *Voila*, madame. There are now two who are on their way. If madame has curiosity, it is easy to follow them."

"But the City of the Sun? What is that? Do you mean Paris?"

"No, madame. It is a mockery like the '*cachemire d'osier*.' You will see."

It is in this following that the polished veneer which makes the outward Paris showed what may lie beneath. Certainly, no one who walks through the Avenue Victor Hugo, one of the twelve avenues radiating from the Arc de Triomphe, and including some of the gayest and most brilliant life of modern Paris, the creation of Napoleon III. and of Baron Haussman, would dream that hint of corruption could enter in. The ancient Rue de la Révolte has changed form and title, and the beautiful avenue is no dishonor to its present name. But far down there opens nearly imperceptibly a narrow alley almost subterranean, and it is through this alley that the two figures which had moved silently down the avenue passed and went on; the man solid and compact, as if well-fed, his face as he turned, however, giving the lie to such impression, but his keen alert eyes seeing every shade of difference in the merest scrap of calico or tufts of hair. For the woman, it was plain to see why the needle had been of small service, her wandering, undecided blue eyes passing over everything to which the man's hook had not first directed her.

Through the narrow way the pair passed into a sombre court, closed at the end by a door of wood with rusty latch, which creaks and objects as one seeks to lift it. Once within, and the door closed, the place has no reminder of the Paris just without. On the contrary, it might be a bit from the beggars' quarter in a village of Syria or Palestine, for here is only a line of flat-roofed huts, the walls whitewashed, the floors level with the soil, and the sun of the warm spring day pouring down upon sleeping dogs, and heaps of refuse alternating with piles of rags, in the midst of which work two or three women, silent at present, and barely looking up as the new comers lay down their burdens. A fat yet acrid odor rises about these huts, drawn out from the rags by the afternoon heat; yet, repulsive as it is, there is more sense of cleanliness about it than in the hideous basements where the same trade is plied in London or New York. There is a space here not yet occupied by buildings. The line of huts faces the south; a fence encloses them; and so silent and alone seems the spot that it is easy to understand why it bears its own individual name, and to the colony of *chiffoniers* who dwell here has long been known as the City of the Sun. Doors stand open freely; honesty is a tradition of this profession; and the police know that these delvers in dust heaps will bring to them any precious object found therein, and that he who should remove the slightest article from one of these dwellings would be banished ignominiously and deprived of all rights of association.

These huts are all alike; two rooms, the larger reserved for the bed, the smaller for kitchen, and in both rags of every variety. In the corner is a heap chiefly of silk, wool, and linen. This is the pile from which rent is to come, and every precious bit goes to it, since rent here is paid in advance,—three francs a week for the hut alone, and twenty francs a month if a scrap of court is added in which the rags can be sorted. On a fixed day the proprietor appears, and, if the sum is not ready, simply carries off the door and windows, and expels the unlucky tenant with no further formality. How the stipulated amount is scraped together, only the half-starved *chiffoniers* know, since prices have fallen so that the hundred kilogrammes (about two hundred pounds) of rags, which, before the war, sold for eighty francs, to-day bring precisely eight.

"In a good day, madame," said the woman, "we can earn three francs. We are always together, I and my man, and we never cease. But the dead season comes, that is, the summer, when Paris is in the country or at the sea; then we can earn never more than two francs, and often not more than thirty sous, when they clean the streets so much, and so carry away everything that little is left for us. It is five years that I have followed my man, and he is born to it, and works always, but the time is changed. There is no more a living in this, or in anything we can do. I have gone hungry when it is the sewing that I do, and I go hungry now, but I am not alone. It is so for all of us, and we care not if only the children are fed. They are not, and it is because of them that we suffer. See, madame, this is the child of my niece, who came with me here, and has also her man, but never has any one of them eaten to the full, even of crusts, which often are in what we gather."

The child ran toward her,—a girl three or four years old, wearing a pair of women's shoes ten times too large, and the remainder of a chemise. Other clothing had not been attempted, or was not considered necessary, and the child looked up with hollow eyes and a face pinched and sharpened by want, while the swollen belly of the meagre little figure showed how wretched had been the supply they called food. All day these children fare as they can, since all day the parents must range the streets collecting their harvest; but fortunately for such future as they can know, these little savages, fighting together like wild animals, have within the last twenty years been gradually gathered into free schools, the work beginning with a devoted woman, who, having seen the City of the Sun, never rested till a school was opened for its children. All effort, however, was quite fruitless, till an old *chiffonier*, also once a seamstress, united with her, and persuaded the mothers that they must prepare their children, or, at least, not prevent them from going. At present the school stands as one of the wisest philanthropies of Paris, but neither this, nor any other attempt to better conditions, alters the fact that twelve and fourteen hours of labor have for sole result from thirty to forty sous a day, and that this sum represents the earnings of the average women-workers of Paris, the better class of trades and occupations being no less limited in possibilities.

CHAPTER XVII.

DRESSMAKERS AND MILLINERS IN PARIS.

"If a revolution come again, I think well, madame, it will be the great shops that will fall, and that it is workwomen who will bear the torch and even consent to the name of terror, *pétroleuses*. For see a moment what thing they do, madame. Everywhere, the girl who desires to learn as *modiste*, and who, in the day when I had learned, became one of the house that she served, and, if talent were there, could rise and in time be mistress herself, with a name that had fame even,—that girl must now attempt the great shop and bury her talent in always the same thing. No more invention, no more grace, but a hundred robes always the same, and with no mark of difference for her who wears it, or way to tell which may be mistress and which the servant. It is not well for one or the other, madame; it is ill for both. Then, too, many must stand aside who would learn, since it is always the machine to sew that needs not many. It is true there are still houses that care for a name, and where one may be *artiste*, and have pride in an inspiration. But they are rare; and now one sits all day, and this one stitches sleeves, perhaps, or seams of waists or skirts, and knows not effects, or how to plan the whole, or any joy of composition or result. It is bad, and all bad, and I willingly would see the great shops go, and myself urge well their destruction."

These words, and a flood of more in the same direction, came as hot protest against any visit to the Magasins du Louvre, an enormous establishment of the same order as the Bon Marché, but slightly higher in price, where hundreds are employed as saleswomen, and where, side by side with the most expensive productions of French skill, are to be found the *occasions*, —the bargains in which the foreigner delights even more than the native.

"Let them go there," pursued the little *modiste*, well on in middle life, whose eager face and sad dark eyes lighted with indignation as she spoke. "Let those go there who have money, always money, but no taste, no perception, no feeling for a true combination. I know that if one orders a robe that one comes to regard to say, 'Yes, so and so must be for madame,' but how shall she know well when she is blunted and dead with numbers? How shall she feel what is best? I, madame, when one comes to me, I study. There are many things that make the suitability of a confection; there is not only complexion and figure and age, but when I have said all these, the thought that blends the whole and sees arising what must be for the perfect robe. This was the method of Madame Desmoulins, and I have learned of her. When it is an important case, a trousseau perhaps, she has neither eaten nor slept till she has conceived her list and sees each design clear. And then what joy! She selects, she blends with tears of happiness; she cuts with solemnity even. Is there such a spirit in your Bon Marché? Is there such a spirit anywhere but here and there to one who remembers; who has an ideal and who refuses to make it less by selling it in the shops? Again, madame, I tell you it is a debasement so to do. I will none of it."

Madame, who had clasped her hands and half risen in her excited protest, sank back in her chair and fixed her eyes on a robe just ready to send home, —a creation so simply elegant and so charming that her brow smoothed and she smiled, well pleased. But her words were simply the echo of others of the same order, spoken by others who had watched the course of women's occupations and who had actual love for the profession they had chosen.

Questions brought out a state of things much the same for both Paris and London, where the system of learning the business had few differences. For both millinery and dressmaking, apprenticeship had been the rule, the more important houses taking an entrance fee and lessening the number of years required; the others demanding simply the full time of the learner, from two to four years. In these latter cases food and lodging were given, and after the first six months a small weekly wage, barely sufficient to provide the Sunday food and lodging. If more was paid, the learner lived outside entirely; and the first year or two was a sharp struggle to make ends meet. But if any talent showed itself, promotion was rapid, and with it the prospect of independence in the end, the directress of a group of girls regarding such talent as developed by the house and a part of its reputation. In some cases such girls by the end of the third year received often five or six thousand francs, and in five were their own mistresses absolutely, with an income of ten or twelve thousand and often more.

This for the exception; for the majority was the most rigid training,—with its result in what we know as French finish, which is simply delicate painstaking with every item of the work,—and a wage of from thirty to forty francs a week, often below but seldom above this sum.

In the early stages of the apprenticeship there was simply an allowance of from six to ten francs per month for incidental expenses, and even when skill increased and services became valuable, five francs a week was considered an ample return. In all these cases the week passed under the roof of the employer, and Sunday alone became the actual change of the worker. The excessive hours of the London apprentice had no counterpart here or had not until the great houses were founded and steam and electric power came with the sewing-machine. With this new regime over-time was often claimed, and two sous an hour allowed, these being given in special cases. But exhausting hours were left for the lower forms of needle-work. The food provided was abundant and good, and sharp overseer as madame might prove, she demanded some relaxation for herself and allowed it to her employés. The different conditions of life made over-work in Paris a far different thing from over-work in London. For both milliners and *modistes* was the keen ambition to develop a talent, and the workroom, as has already been stated, felt personal pride in any member of the force who showed special lightness of touch or skill in combination.

"Work, madame!" exclaimed little Madame M., as she described a day's work under the system which had trained her. "But yes, I could not so work now, but then I saw always before me an end. I had the sentiment. It was always that the colors arranged themselves, and so with my sister, who is *modiste* and whose compositions are a marvel. My back has ached, my eyes have burned, I have seen sparks before them and have felt that I could no more, when the days are long and the heat perhaps is great, or even in winter crowded together and the air so heavy. But we laughed and sang; we thought of a future; we watched for talent, and if there was envy or jealousy, it was well smothered. I remember one talented Italian who would learn and who hated one other who had great gifts; hated her so, she has stabbed her suddenly with sharp scissors in the arm. But such things are not often. We French care always for genius, even if it be but to make a shoe most perfect, and we do not hate—no, we love well, whoever shows it. But to-day all is different, and once more I say, madame, that too much is made, and that thus talent will die and gifts be no more needed."

There is something more in this feeling than the mere sense of rivalry or money loss from the new system represented by the Bon Marché and other great establishments of the same nature. But this is a question in one sense apart from actual conditions, save as the concentration of labor has had its effect on the general rate of wages. Five francs a day is considered riches, and the ordinary worker or assistant in either dressmaking or millinery department receives from two and a half to three and a half francs, on which sum she must subsist as she can. With a home where earnings go into a common fund, or if the worker has no one dependent upon her, French thrift makes existence on this sum quite possible; but when it becomes a question of children to be fed and clothed, more than mere existence is impossible, and starvation stands always in the background. For the younger workers the great establishments, offer many advantages over the old system, and hours have been shortened and attempts made in a few cases to improve general conditions of those employed. But there is always a dull season, in which wages lessen, or even cease for a time, the actual number of working days averaging two hundred and eighty. Where work is private and reputation is established, the year's earnings are a matter of individual ability, but the mass of workers in these directions drift naturally toward the great shops which may be found now in every important street of Paris, and which have altered every feature of the old system. Whether this alteration is a permanent one, is a question to which no answer can yet be made. Wages have reached a point barely above subsistence, and the outlook for the worker is a very shadowy one; but the question as a whole has as yet small interest for any but the political economists, while the women themselves have no thought of organization or of any method of bettering general conditions, beyond the little societies to which some of the ordinary workers belong, and which are half religious, half educational, in their character. As a rule, these are for the lower ranks of needlewomen, but necessity will compel something more definite in form for the two classes we have been considering, as well as for those below them, and the time approaches when this will be plain to the workers themselves, and some positive action take the place of the present dumb acceptance of whatever comes.

CHAPTER XVIII.

A SILK-WEAVER OF PARIS.

"No, madame, there is no more any old Paris. The Paris that I remember is gone, all gone, save here and there a corner that soon they will pull down as all the rest. All changes, manners no less than these streets that I know not in their new dress, and where I go seeking a trace of what is past. It is only in the churches that one feels that all is the same, and even with them one wonders why, if it is the same, fewer and fewer come, and that men smile often at those that enter the doors, and would close them to us who still must pray in the old places. Is there that consolation for the worker in America, madame? Can she forget her sorrow and want at a shrine that is holy, and feel the light resting on her, full of the glory of the painted windows and the color that is joy and rest? Because, if there had not been the church, my St. Etienne du Mont, that I know from a child, if there had not been that, I must have died. And so I have wondered if your country had this gift also for the worker, and, if it has not bread enough, has at least something that feeds the soul. Is it so, madame?"

Poor old Rose, once weaver in silk and with cheeks like her name, looking at me now with her sad eyes, blue and clear still in spite of her almost seventy years, and full of the patience born of long struggle and acceptance! St. Etienne had drawn me as it had drawn her, and it was in the apse, the light streaming from the ancient windows, each one a marvel of color whose secret no man to-day has penetrated, that I saw first the patient face and the clasped hands of this suppliant, who prayed there undisturbed by any thought of watching eyes, and who rose presently and went slowly down the aisles, with a face that might have taken its place beside the pictured saints to whom she had knelt. Her *sabots* clicked against the pavement worn by many generations of feet, and her old fingers still moved mechanically, telling the beads which she had slipped out of sight.

"You love the little church," I said; and she answered instantly, with a smile that illumined the old face, "Indeed, yes; and why not? It is home and all that is good, and it is so beautiful, madame. There is none like it. I go to the others sometimes, above all to Nôtre Dame, which also is venerable and dear, and where one may worship well. But always I return here; for the great church seems to carry my prayers away, and they are half lost in such bigness, and it is not so bright and so joyous as this. For here the color lifts the heart, and I seem to rise in my soul also, and I know every pillar and ornament, for my eyes study often when my lips pray; but it is all one worship, madame, else I should shut them close. But the good God and the saints know well that I am always praying, and that it is my St. Etienne that helps, and that is so beautiful I must pray when I see it."

This was the beginning of knowing Rose, and in good time her whole story was told,—a very simple one, but a record that stands for many like it. There was neither discontent nor repining. Born among workers, she had filled her place, content to fill it, and only wondering as years went on why there were not better days, and, if they were to mend for others, whether she had part in it or not. Far up under the roof of an old house, clung to because it was old, Rose climbed, well satisfied after the minutes in the little church in which she laid down the burden that long ago had become too heavy for her, and which, if it returned at all, could always be dropped again at the shrine which had heard her first prayer.

"It is Paris that I know best," she said, "and that I love always, but I am not born in it, nor none of mine. It is my father that desired much that we should gain more, and who is come here when I am so little that I can be carried on the back. He is a weaver, madame, a weaver of silk, and my mother knows silk also from the beginning. Why not, when it is to her mother who also has known it, and she winds cocoons, too, when she is little? I have played with them for the first plaything, and indeed the only one, madame, since, when I learn what they are and how one must use them, I have knowledge enough to hold the threads, and so begin. It was work, yes, but not the work of to-day. We worked together. If my father brought us here, it was that all things might be better; for he loved us well. He sang as he wove, and we sang with him. If hands were tired, he said always: 'Think how you are earning for us all, and for the *dot* that some day you shall have when your blue eyes are older, and some one comes who will see that they are wise eyes that, if they laugh, know also all the ways that these threads must go.' That pleased me, for I was learning, too, and together we earned well, and had our *pot au feu* and good wine and no lack of bread.

"That was the hand-loom, and when at last is come another that goes with steam, the weavers have revolted and sworn to destroy them all, since one could do the work of many. I hear it all, and listen, and think how it is that a man's mind can think a thing that takes bread from other men. I am sixteen, then, and skilful and with good wages for every day, and it is then that Armand is come,—Armand, who was weaver, too, but who had been soldier with the great Emperor, and seen the girls of all countries. But he cared for none of them till he saw me, for his thought was always on his work; and he, too, planned machines, and fretted that he had not education enough to make them with drawings and figures so that the masters would understand. When machines have come he has fretted more; for one at least had been clear in his own thought, and now he cannot have it as he will, since another's thought has been before him. He told me all this, believing I could understand; and so I could, madame, since love made me wise enough to see what he might mean, and if I had not words, at least I had ears, and always I have used them well. We are still one family when the time comes that I marry, and my father has good wages in spite of machines, and all are reconciled to them, save my brother. But the owners build factories. It is no longer at home that one can work; and in these the children go, yes, even little ones, and hours are longer, and there is no song to cheer them, and no mother who can speak sometimes or tell a tale as they wind, and all is different. And so my mother says always: 'It is not good for France that the loom is taken out of the houses;' and if she makes more money because of more silk, she loses things that are more precious than money, and it is all bad that it must be so. My father shakes his head. There are wages for every child; and he sees this, and does not so well see that they earned also at home, and had some things that the factory stops, for always.

"For me, I am weaver of ribbons, and I love them well, all the bright, beautiful colors. I look at the windows of my St. Etienne and feel the color like a song in my heart, and while I weave I see them always, and could even think that I spin them from my own mind.

"That is a fancy that has rest when the days are long, and the sound of the mill in my ears, and the beat of the machines, that I feel sometimes are cruel, for one can never stop, but must go on always. I think in myself, as I see the children, that I shall never let mine stand with them, and indeed there is no need, since we are all earning, and there is money saved, and this is all true for long. The children are come. Three boys are mine; two with Armand's eyes, and one with mine, whom Armand loves best because of this, but seeks well to make no difference, and we call him Etienne for my saint and my church. And, madame, I think often that more heaven is in him than we often know, and perhaps because I have prayed always under the window where the lights are all at last one glory, and the color itself is a prayer, Etienne is so born that he must have it, too. I take him there a baby, and he stretches his hands and smiles. He does not shout like the others, but his smile seems from heaven. He is an artist. He draws always with a bit of charcoal, with anything, and I think that he shall study, and, it may be, make other beautiful things that may live in a new St. Etienne, or in some other place in this Paris that I love; and I am happy.

"Then comes the time, madame, that one remembers and prays to forget, till one knows that it may be the good God's way of telling us how wrong we are and what we must learn. First it is Armand, who has become revolutionary,—what you call to-day communist,—and who is found in what are called plots, and tried and imprisoned. It was not for long. He would have come to me again, but the fever comes and kills many; he dies and I cannot be with him,—no, nor even see him when they take him to burial. I go in a dream. I will not believe it; and then my father is hurt. He is caught in one of those machines that my mother so hates, and his hand is gone and his arm crushed.

"Now the children must earn. There is no other way. For Armand and Pierre I could bear it, since they are stronger, but for Etienne, no. He comes from school that he loves, and must take his place behind the loom. He is patient; he says, even, he is glad to earn for us all; but he is pale, and the light in his eyes grows dim, save when, night and morning, he kneels with me under my window and feels it as I do.

"Then evil days are here, and always more and more evil. Month by month wages are less and food is more. My mother is dead, too, and my father quite helpless, and my brother that has never been quite as others, and so cannot earn. We work always. My boys know well all that must be known, but at seventeen Armand is tall and strong as a man, and he is taken for soldier, and he, too, never comes to us again. I work more and more, and if I earn two francs for the day am glad, but now Etienne is sick and I see well that he cannot escape. 'It is the country he needs,' says the doctor. 'He must be taken to the country if he is to live;' but these are words. I pray,—I pray always that succor may come, but it comes not, nor can I even be with him in his pain, since I must work always. And so it is, madame, that one day when I return, my father lies on his bed weeping, and the priest is there and looks with pity upon me, and my Etienne lies there still, and the smile that was his only is on his face.

"That is all, madame. My life has ended there. But it goes on for others still and can. My father has lived till I too am almost old. My brother lives yet, and my boy, Pierre, who was shot at Balaklava, he has two children and his wife, who is *couturière*, and I must aid them. I remain weaver, and I earn always the same. Wages stay as in the beginning, but all else is more and more. One may live, but that is all. Many days we have only bread; sometimes not enough even of that. But the end comes. I have always my St. Etienne, and often under the window I see my Etienne's smile, and know well the good God has cared for him, and I need no more. I could wish only that the children might be saved, but I cannot tell. France needs them; but I think well she needs them more as souls than as hands that earn wages, though truly I am old and it may be that I do not know what is best. Tell me, madame, must the children also work always with you, or do you care for other things than work, and is there time for one to live and grow as a plant in the sunshine? That is what I wish for the children; but Paris knows no such life, nor can it, since we must live, and so I must wait, and that is all."

CHAPTER XIX.

IN THE RUE JEANNE D'ARC.

"No, madame, unless one has genius or much money in the beginning, it is only possible to live, and sometimes one believes that it is not living. If it were not that all in Paris is so beautiful, how would I have borne much that I have known? But always, when even the hunger has been most sharp, has been the sky so blue and clear, and the sun shining down on the beautiful boulevards, and all so bright, so gay, why should I show a face of sorrow?

"I have seen the war, it is true. I have known almost the starving, for in those days all go hungry; most of all, those who have little to buy with. But one bears the hunger better when one has been born to it, and that is what has been for me.

"In the Rue Jeanne d'Arc we are all hungry, and it is as true to-day, yes, more true, than in the days when I was young. The charitable, who give more and more each year in Paris, will not believe there is such a quarter, but for us, we know. Have you seen the Rue Jeanne d'Arc, madame? Do you know what can be for this Paris that is so fair?"

This question came in the square before old Nôtre Dame, still the church of the poor, its gray towers and carved portals dearer to them than to the Paris which counts the Madeleine a far better possession than this noblest of all French cathedrals. Save for such reminder this quarter might have remained unvisited, since even philanthropic Paris appears to have little or no knowledge of it, and it is far beyond the distance to which the most curious tourist is likely to penetrate.

On by the Halle aux Vins, with its stifling, fermenting, alcoholic odors, and then by the Jardin des Plantes, and beyond, the blank walls of many manufactories stretching along the Seine,—this for one shore. On the other lies La Rapée, with the windows of innumerable wine shops flaming in the sun, and further on, Bercy, the ship bank of the river, covered with wine-casks and a throng of drays and draymen; of *débardeurs*, whose business it is to unload wood or to break up old boats into material for kindling; and of the host whose business is on and about the river.

They are of the same order as the London Dock laborers, and, like the majority of this class there and here, know every extremity of want. But it is a pretty picture from which one turns from the right, passing up the noisy boulevard of the Gare d'Orléans, toward the quarter of the Gobelins. This quarter has its independent name and place like the "City of the Sun." Like that it knows every depth of poverty, but, unlike that, sunshine and space are quite unknown. The buildings are piled together, great masses separated by blind alleys, some fifteen hundred lodgings in all, and the owner of many of them is a prominent philanthropist, whose name heads the list of directors for various charitable institutions, but whose feet, we must believe, can hardly be acquainted with those alleys and stairways, narrow, dark, and foul. The unpaved ways show gaping holes in which the greasy mud lies thick or mingles with the pools of standing water, fed from every house and fermenting with rottenness.

The sidewalks, once asphalted, are cracked in long seams and holes, where the same water does its work, and where hideous exhalations poison the air. Within it is still worse; filth trickles down the walls and mingles under foot, the corridors seeming rather sewers than passages for human beings, while the cellars are simply reservoirs for the same deposits. Above in the narrow rooms huddle the dwellers in those lodgings; whole families in one room, its single window looking on a dark court where one sees swarms of half-naked children, massed together like so many maggots, their flabby flesh a dirty white, their faces prematurely aged and with a diabolical intelligence in their sharp eyes. The children are always old. The old have reached the extremity of hideous decrepitude. One would say that these veins had never held healthy human blood, and that for young and old pus had become its substitute. To these homes return many of the men who wait for work on the quays, and thus this population, born to crime and every foulness that human life can know, has its proportion also of honest workers, whose fortunes have ebbed till they have been left stranded in this slime, of a quality so tenacious that escape seems impossible. Many of the lodgings are unoccupied, and at night they become simply dens of wild beasts,—men and boys who live by petty thieving climbing the walls, stealing along the passages and up the dark stairways, and sheltering themselves in every niche and corner. Now and then, when the outrages become too evident, the police descend suddenly on the drinking, shouting tenants at will, and for a day or two there is peace for the rest.

But the quarter is shut in and hedged about by streets of a general respectable appearance, and thus it is felt to be impossible that such a spot can exist. It is, however, the breeding-ground of criminals; and each year swells the quota, whose lives can have but one ending, and who cost the city in the end many times the amount that in the beginning would have insured decent homes and training in an industrial school.

It is only the dregs of humanity that remain in such quarters. The better elements, unless compelled by starvation, flee from it, though with the tenacity of the Parisian for his own *quartier*, they settle near it still. All about are strange trades, invented often by the followers of them, and unknown outside a country which has learned every method of not only turning an honest penny, but doing it in the most effective way. Among them all not one can be stranger than that adopted by Madame Agathe, whose soft voice and plaintive intonations are in sharpest contrast with her huge proportions, and who began life as one of the great army of *couturières*.

With failing eyesight and the terror of starvation upon her, she went one Sunday, with her last two francs in her pocket, to share them with a sick cousin, who had been one of the workmen at the Jardin des Plantes. He, too, was in despair; for an accident had taken from him the use of his right arm, and there were two children who must be fed.

"What to do! what to do!" he cried; and then, as he saw the tears running down Madame Agathe's cheeks, he in turn, with the ease of his nation, wept also.

"That is what has determined me," said Madame Agathe, as not long ago she told of the day when she had given up hope. "Tears are for women, and even for them it is not well to shed many. I say to myself, 'I am on the earth: the good God wills it. There must be something that I may do, and that will help these even more helpless ones.' And as I say it there comes in from the Jardin des Plantes a man who has been a companion to Pierre, and who, as he sees him so despairing, first embraces him and then tells him this:

'Pierre, it is true you cannot again hold spade or hoe, but here is something. There are never enough ants' eggs for the zoölogical gardens and for those that feed pheasants. I know already one woman who supplies them, and she will some day be rich. Why not you also?'

"'I have no hands for any work. This hand is useless,' said Pierre; and then I spoke: 'But mine are here and are strong; you have eyes, which for me are well nigh gone. It shall be your eyes and my hands that will do this work if I may learn all the ways. It is only that ants have teeth and bite and we must fear that.'

"Then Claude has laughed. 'Teeth! yes, if you will, but they do not gnaw like hunger. Come with me, Madame Agathe, and we will talk with her of whom I speak,—she who knows it all and has the good heart and will tell and help.'

"That is how I begun, madame. It is Blanche who has taught me, and I have lived with her a month and watched all her ways, and learned all that these ants can do. At first one must renounce thought to be anything but bitten, yes, bitten always. See me, I am tanned as leather. It is the skin of an apple that has dried that you see on me and with her it is the same. We wear pantaloons and gauntlets of leather. It is almost a coat of mail, but close it as one may, they are always underneath. She can sleep when hundreds run on her, but I, I am frantic at first till I am bitten everywhere; and then, at last, as with bee-keepers, I can be poisoned no longer, and they may gnaw as they will. They are very lively. They love the heat, and we must keep up great heat always and feed them very high, and then they lay many eggs, which we gather for the bird-breeders and others who want them. Twice we have been forced to move, since our ants will wander, and the neighbors complain when their pantries are full, and justly.

"Now eight and even ten sacks of ants come to me from Germany and many places. I am busy always, and there is money enough for all; but I have sent the children away, for they are girls, and for each I save a little *dot*, and I will not have them know this *métier*, and be so bitten that they, too, are tanned like me and have never more their pretty fresh skins. Near us now, madame, is another woman, but her trade is less good than mine. She is a bait-breeder, '*une éleveure des asticots*.' All about her room hang old stockings. In them she puts bran and flour and bits of cork, and soon the red worms show themselves, and once there she has no more thought than to let them grow and to sell them for eight and sometimes ten sous a hundred. But I like better my ants, which are clean, and which, if they run everywhere, do not wriggle nor squirm nor make you think always of corruption and death. She breeds other worms for the fishermen, who buy them at the shops for fishing tackle; but often she also buys worms from others and feeds them a little time till plump, but I find them even more disgusting.

"An ant has so much intelligence. I can watch mine, madame, as if they were people almost, and would even believe they know me. But that does not hinder them from biting me; no, never; and because they are always upon me the neighbors and all who know me have chosen to call me the 'sister-in-law of ants.'

"It is not a trade for women, it is true, save for one only here and there. But it is better than sewing; yes, far better; and I wish all women might have something as good, since now I prosper when once I ate only bread. What shall be done, madame, to make it that more than bread becomes possible for these workers?"

CHAPTER XX.

FROM FRANCE TO ITALY.

In Paris, its fulness of brilliant life so dominates that all shadows seem to fly before it and poverty and pain to have no place, and the same feeling holds for the chief cities of the continent. It is Paris that is the key-note of social life, and in less degree its influence makes itself felt even at remote distances, governing production and fixing the rate of wages paid. Modern improvement has swept away slums, and it is only here and there, in cities like Berlin or Vienna, that one comes upon anything which deserves the name.

The Ghetto is still a part of Rome, and likely to remain so, since the conservatism of the lowest order is stronger even in the Italian than in the French or German worker.

But if civilization does not abolish the effects of low wages and interminable hours of labor, it at least removes them from sight, and having made its avenues through what once were dens, is certain that all dens are done away with. The fact that the avenue is made, that sunshine enters dark courts and noisome alleys, and that often court and alley are swept away absolutely, is a step gained; yet, as is true of Shaftesbury Avenue in London cut through the old quarters of St. Giles, the squalor and misery is condensed instead of destroyed, and the building that held one hundred holds now double or triple that number. For Paris the Rue Jeanne d'Arc already described is an illustration of what may lie within a stone's throw of quiet and reputable streets, and of what chances await the worker, whose scanty wages offer only existence, and for whom the laying up of any fund for old age is an impossibility.

The chief misfortune, however, and one mourned by the few French political economists who have looked below the surface, is the gradual disappearance of family life and its absorption into that of the factory.

With this absorption has come other vices, that follow where the family has no further place, and, recognizing this at last, the heads of various great manufactories—notably in Lyons and other points where the silk industry centres—have sought to reorganize labor as much as possible on the family basis. In the old days, when the loom was a part of the furniture of every home, the various phases of weaving were learned one by one, and the child who began by filling bobbins, passed on gradually to the mastery of every branch involved, and became judge of qualities as well as maker of quantities. In this phase, if hours were long, there were at least the breaks of the ordinary family life,—the care of details taken by each in turn, and thus a knowledge acquired, which, with the development of the factory system on its earliest basis, was quite impossible. There were other alleviations, too, as the store of songs and of traditions testifies, both these possibilities ceasing when home labor was transferred to the factory.

On the other hand, there were certain compensations, in the fixing of a definite number of hours, of the rate of wages, and at first in freeing the home from the workshop element, the loom having usurped the largest and best place in every household. But, as machinery developed, the time of mother and children was again absorbed, and so absolutely that any household knowledge ended then and there, with no further possibility of its acquisition. It was this state of things, with its accumulated results, which, a generation or so later, faced the few investigators who puzzled over the decadence of morals, the enfeebled physiques, the general helplessness of the young women who married, and the whole series of natural consequences. So startling were the facts developed, that it became at once evident that a change must be brought about, if only as a measure of wise political economy; and thus it has happened for Lyons that the factory system has perfected itself, and matches or even goes beyond that of any other country, with the exception of isolated points like Saltaire in England, or the Chenney village in Connecticut. When it became evident that the ordinary factory girl-worker at sixteen or seventeen could not sew a seam, or make a broth, or care for a child's needs so well as the brute, the time for action had come; and schools of various orders, industrial and otherwise, have gradually risen and sought to undo the work of the years that made them necessary. Perfect in many points as the system has become, however, competition has so followed and pressed upon the manufacturer that the wage standard has lowered to little more than subsistence point, this fact including all forms of woman's work, without the factory as well as within.

Leaving France and Germany and looking at Swiss and Italian workers, much the same statements may be made, the lace-workers in Switzerland, for instance, being an illustration of the very minimum of result for human labor. Like the lace-workers of Germany, the fabric must often grow in the dark almost, basements being chosen that dampness may make the thread follow more perfectly the will of the worker, whose day is never less than fifteen hours long, whose food seldom goes beyond black bread with occasional milk or cabbage soup, and whose average of life seldom exceeds forty years. There is not a thread in the exquisite designs that has not been spun from a human nerve stretched to its utmost tension, and the face of these workers once seen are a shadow forever on the lovely webs that every woman covets instinctively.

Why an industry demanding so many delicate qualities—patience, perfection of touch, and long practice—should represent a return barely removed from starvation, no man has told us; but so the facts are, and so they stand for every country of Europe where the work is known. In Germany and Italy alike, the sewing-machine has found its way even to the remotest village, manufacturers in the large towns finding it often for their interest to send their work to points where the lowest rate possible in cities seems to the simple people far beyond what they would dream of asking. It is neither in attic nor basement that the Italian worker runs her machine, but in the open doorway, or even the street itself, sunshine pouring upon her, neighbors chatting in the pauses for basting or other preparation, and the sense of human companionship and interest never for an instant lost. For the Anglo-Saxon such methods are alien to every instinct. For the Italian they are as natural as the reverse would be unnatural; and thus, even with actual wage conditions at the worst, the privations and suffering, which are as inevitable for one as the other, are made bearable, and even sink out of sight almost. They are very tangible facts, but they have had to mean something very near starvation before the Italian turned his face toward America,—the one point where, it is still believed, the worker can escape such fear.

It is hard for the searcher into these places to realize that suffering in any form can have place under such sunshine, or with the apparent joyousness of Italian life; and it is certain that this life holds a compensation unknown to the North.

In Genoa, late in May, I paused in one of the old streets leading up from the quays, where hundreds of sailors daily come and go, and where one of the chief industries for women is the making of various forms of sailor garments. Every doorway opening on the street held its sewing-machine or the low table where cutters and basters were at work, fingers and tongues flying in concert, and a babel of happy sound issuing between the grand old walls of houses seven and eight stories high, flowers in every window, many-colored garments waving from lines stretched across the front, and, far above, a proud mother handing her *bambino* across for examination by her opposite neighbor, a very simple operation where streets are but four or five feet wide.

Life here is reduced to its simplest elements. Abstemious to a degree impossible in a more northern climate, the Italian worker in town or village demands little beyond macaroni, polenta, or chestnuts, with oil or soup, and wine as the occasional luxury; and thus a woman who works fourteen or even fifteen hours a day for a lire and a half, and at times only a lire (20c.), still has enough for absolute needs, and barely looks beyond.

It is only when the little bundle has ceased to be *bambino* that she thinks of a larger life as possible, or wonders why women who work more hours than men, and often do a man's labor, are paid only half the men's rate.

In Rome, where these lines are written, the story is the same. There are few statistics from which one can glean any definite idea of numbers, or even of occupations. The army swallows all the young men, precisely as in France; but women slip less readily into responsible positions, and thus earn in less degree than in either France or Germany.

In the Ghetto swarm the crowds that have filled it for hundreds of years, and its narrow ways hold every trade known to man's hands, as well as every form of drudgery which here reaches its climax.

The church has decreed the relieving of poverty as one chief method of saving rich men's souls, and thus the few attempts made by the English colony to bring about some reconstruction of methods as well as thought have met with every possible opposition, till, within recent years, the necessity of industrial education has become apparent, and Italy has inaugurated some of the best work in this direction. Beyond Italy there has been no attempt at experiment. The work at best has been chiefly from the outside; but whether in this form, or assisted by actual statistics or the general investigation of others, the conclusion is always the same, and sums up as the demand for every worker and every master the resurrection of the old ideal of work; the doing away of competition as it at present rules, and the substitution of co-operation, productive as well as distributive; industrial education for every child, rich or poor; and that and recognition of the interests of all as a portion of our personal charge and responsibility, which, if I name it Socialism, will be scouted as a dream of an impossible future, but which none the less bears that name in its highest interpretation, and is the one solution for every problem on either side the great sea, between the eastern and western worker.

CHAPTER XXI.

PRESENT AND FUTURE.

At the first glance, and even when longer survey has been made, both Paris and Berlin,—and these may stand as the representative Continental cities,—seem to offer every possible facility for the work of women. Everywhere, behind counter, in shop or café, in the markets, on the streets, wherever it is a question of any phase of the ordinary business of life, women are in the ascendant, and would seem to have conquered for themselves a larger place and better opportunities than either England or America have to show. But, as investigation goes on, this larger employment makes itself evident as obstacle rather than help to the better forms of work, and the woman's shoulders bear not only her natural burden, but that also belonging to the man. The army lays its hand on the boy at sixteen or seventeen. The companies and regiments perpetually moving from point to point in Paris seem to be composed chiefly of boys; every student is enrolled, and the period of service must always be deducted in any plan for life made by the family.

Naturally, then, these gaps are filled by women,—not only in all ordinary avocations, but in the trades which are equally affected by this perpetual drain. In every town of France or Germany where manufacturing is of old or present date, the story is the same, and women are the chief workers; but, in spite of this fact, the same inequalities in wages prevail that are found in England and America, while conditions include every form of the sharpest privation.

For England and America as well is the fact that law regulates or seeks to regulate every detail, no matter how minute, and that the manufacturer or artisan of any description is subject to such laws. On the continent, save where gross wrongs have brought about some slight attempt at regulation by the State, the law is merely a matter of general principles, legislation simply indicating certain ends to be accomplished, but leaving the means entirely in the hands of the heads of industries. Germany has a far more clearly defined code than France; but legislation, while it has touched upon child labor, has neglected that of women-workers entirely. Within a year or two the report of the Belgian commissioners has shown a state of things in the coal mines, pictured with tremendous power by Zola in his novel "Germinal," but in no sense a new story, since the conditions of Belgian workers are practically identical with those of women-workers in Silesia, or at any or all of the points on the continent where women are employed. Philanthropists have cried out; political economists have shown the suicidal nature of non-interference, and demonstrated that if the State gains to-day a slight surplus in her treasury, she has, on the other hand, lost something for which no money equivalent can be given, and that the women who labor from twelve to sixteen hours in the mines, or at any industry equally confining, have no power left to shape the coming generations into men, but leave to the State an inheritance of weak-bodied and often weak-minded successors to the same toil. For France and Germany, Belgium, Switzerland, at every point where women are employed, the story is the same; and the fact remains that, while in the better order of trades women may prosper, in the large proportion, constant and exhausting labor simply keeps off actual starvation, but has no margin for anything that can really be called living.

For Paris and Berlin, but in greater degree for Paris, a fact holds true which has almost equal place for New York. Women-workers, whose only support is the needle, contend with an army of women for whom such work is not a support, but who follow it as a means of increasing an already certain income. For these women there is no pressing necessity, and in Paris they are of the *bourgeoisie*, whose desires are always a little beyond their means, who have ungratified caprices, ardent wishes to shine like women in the rank above them, to dress, and to fascinate. They are the wives and daughters of petty clerks, or employés of one order and another, of small government functionaries and the like, who embroider or sew three or four hours a day, and sell the work for what it will bring. The money swells the housekeeping fund, gives a dinner perhaps, or aids in buying a shawl, or some coveted and otherwise unattainable bit of jewelry. The work is done secretly, since they have not the simplicity either of the real *ouvrière* or of the *grande dame*, both of whom sew openly, the one for charity, the other for a living. But this middle class, despising the worker and aspiring always toward the luxurious side of life, feels that embroidery or tapestry of some description is the only suitable thing for their fingers, and busy on this, preserve the appearance of the dignity they covet. Often their yearly gains are not more than one hundred francs, and they seldom exceed two hundred; for they accept whatever is offered them, and the merchants who deal with them know that they submit to any extortion so long as their secret is kept.

This class is one of the obstacles in the way of the ordinary worker, and one that grows more numerous with every year of the growing love of luxury. There must be added to it another,—and in Paris it is a very large one,—that that of women who have known better days, who are determined to keep up appearances and to hide their misery absolutely from former friends. They are timid to excess, and spend days of labor on a piece of work which, in the end, brings them hardly more than a morsel of bread. One who goes below the surface of Paris industries is amazed to discover how large a proportion of women-workers come under this head; and their numbers have been one of the strongest arguments for industrial education, and some development of the sense of what value lies in good work of any order. In one industry alone,—that of bonnet-making in general, it was found a year or two since that over eight hundred women of this order were at work secretly, and though they are found in several other industries, embroidery is their chief source of income. Thus they are in one sense a combination against other women, and one more reason given by merchants of every order for the unequal pay of men and women. It is only another confirmation of the fact that, so long as women are practically arrayed against women, any adjustment of the questions involved in all work is impossible. Hours, wages, all the points at issue that make up the sum of wrong represented by many phases of modern industry, wait for the organization among women themselves; and such organization is impossible till the sense of kinship and mutual obligation has been born. With competition as the heart of every industry, men are driven apart by a force as inevitable and irresistible as its counterpart in the material world, and it is only when an experiment like that of Guise has succeeded, and the patient work and waiting of Père Godin borne fruit that all men pronounce good, that we know what possibilities lie in industrial co-operation. Such co-operation as has there proved itself not only possible but profitable for every member concerned, comes at last, to one who has faced women-workers in every trade they count their own, and under every phase of want and misery, born of ignorance first, and then of the essential conditions of competition, under-pay, and over-work, as one great hope for the future. The instant demand, if it is to become possible, is for an education sufficiently technical to give each member of society the hand-skill necessary to make a fair livelihood. Such knowledge is impossible without perfectly equipped industrial schools; and the need of these has so demonstrated itself that further argument for their adoption is hardly necessary. The constant advance in invention and the fact that the worker, unless exceptionally skilled, is more and more the servant of machinery, is an appeal no less powerful in the same direction. Twenty years ago one of the wisest thinkers in France, conservative, yet with the clearest sense of what the future must bring for all workers, wrote:—

> "From the economic point of view, woman, who has next to no material force and whose arms are advantageously replaced by the least machine, can have useful place and obtain fair remuneration only by the development of the best qualities of her intelligence. It is the inexorable law of our civilization—the principle and formula even of social progress, that *mechanical engines are to accomplish every operation of human labor which does not proceed directly from the mind*. The hand of man is each day deprived of a portion of its original task, but this general gain is a loss for the particular, and for the classes whose only instrument of labor and of earning daily bread is a pair of feeble arms."

The machine, the synonym for production at large, has refined and subtilized—even spiritualized itself to a degree almost inconceivable, nor is there any doubt but that the future has far greater surprises in store. But if metal has come to wellnigh its utmost power of service, the worker's capacity has had no equality of development, and the story of labor to-day for the whole working world is one of degradation. That men are becoming alive to this; that students of political economy solemnly warn the producer what responsibility is his; and that the certainty of some instant step as vital and inevitable is plain,—are gleams of light in this murky and sombre sky, from which it would seem at times only the thunderbolt could be certain.

Organization and its result in industrial co-operation is one goal, but even this must count in the end only as corrective and palliative unless with it are associated other reforms which this generation is hardly likely to see, yet which more and more outline themselves as a part of those better days for which we work and hope. As to America thus far, our great spaces, our sense of unlimited opportunity, of the chance for all which we still count as the portion of every one on American soil, and a hundred other standard and little-questioned beliefs, have all seemed testimony to the reality and certainty of our faith. But as one faces the same or worse industrial conditions in London or any great city, English or Continental, with its congestion of labor and its mass of resultant misery, the same solution suggests itself and the cry comes from philanthropist and Philistine alike, "Send them into the country! Give them homes and work there!"

Naturally this would seem the answer; but where? For when search is made for any bit of land on which a home may rise and food be given back from the soil, all England is found to be in the hands of a few thousand land-owners, while London itself practically belongs to less than a dozen, with rents at such rates that when paid no living wage remains. When once this land question is touched, it is found made up of immemorial injustices, absurdities, outrages, and for America no less than for the whole world of workers. It cannot be that man has right to air and sunshine, but never right to the earth under his feet. Standing-place there must be for this long battle for existence, and in yielding this standing-place comes instant solution of a myriad problems.

This is no place for extended argument as to the necessity of land nationalization, or the advantages or disadvantages of Mr. George's scheme of a single tax on land values, with the consequent dropping of our whole complicated tariff. But believing that the experiment is at least worth trying, and trying patiently and thoroughly, the belief, slowly made plain and protested against till further protest became senseless and impossible, stands here, as one more phase of work to be done. In it are bound up many of the reforms, without which the mere fact of granted standing-room would be valueless. The day must come when no one can question that the natural opportunities of life can never rightfully be monopolized by individuals, and when the education that fits for earning, and the means of earning are under wise control, monopolies, combinations, "trusts,"—all the facts which represent organized injustice sink once for all to their own place.

Differ as we may, then, regarding methods and possibilities, one question rises always for every soul alike,—What part have I in this awakening, and what work with hands or head can I do to speed this time to which all men are born, and of which to-day they know only the promise? From lowest to highest, the material side has so dominated that other needs have slipped out of sight; and to-day, often, the hands that follow the machine in its almost human operations, are less human than it. Matter is God, and for scientist and speculative philosopher, and too often for social reformer also, the place and need of another God ceases, and there is no hope for the toiler but to lie down at last in the dust and find it sweet to him. Yet for him, and for each child of man, is something as certain. Not the God of theology; not the God made the fetich and blindly worshipped; but the Power whose essence is love and inward constraint to righteousness, and to whom all men must one day come, no matter through what dark ways or with what stumbling feet.

The vision is plain and clear of what the State must one day mean and what the work of the world must be, when once more the devil of self-seeking and greed flees to his own place, and each man knows that his life is his own only as he gives it to high service, and to loving thought for every weaker soul. The co-operative commonwealth must come; and when it has come, all men will know that it is but the vision of every age in which high souls have seen what future is for every child of man, and have known that when the spirit of brotherhood rules once for all, the city of God has in very truth descended from the heavens, and men at last have found their own inheritance.

This is the future, remote even when most ardently desired; impossible, unless with the dream is bound up the act that brings realization. And when the nature and method of such act comes as question, and the word is, What can be done to-day, in the hour that now is?—how shall unlearned, unthinking minds bend themselves to these problems, when the wisest have failed, and the world still struggles in bondage to custom, the accumulated force of long-tolerated wrong—what can the answer be?

There is no enlightener like even the simplest act of real justice. It is impossible that the most limited mind should not feel expansion and know illumination in even the effort to comprehend what justice actually is and involves. Instantly when its demand is heard and met, custom, tradition, old beliefs, everything that hampers progress, slip away, and actual values show themselves. The first step taken in such direction means always a second. It is the beginning of the real march onward; the ending of any blind drifting in the mass, with no consciousness of individual power to move.

A deep conviction founded on eternal law is itself an education, and whoever has once determined what the personal demand in life is, has entered the wicket-gate and sees before him a plain public road, on which all humanity may journey to the end.

Here then lies the answer, no less than in these last words, the ending of one phase of work which still has only begun. For the day is coming when every child born will be taught the meaning of wealth, of capital, of labor. Then there will be small need of any further schools of political economy, since wealth will be known to be only what the soul can earn,—that which adheres and passes on with it; and capital, all forces that the commonwealth can use to make the man develop to his utmost possibility every power of soul and body; and labor, the joyful, voluntary acceptance of all work to this end, whether with hands or head. Till then, in the fearless and faithful acceptance of every consequence of a conviction, in personal consecration to the highest demand, in increasing effort to make happiness the portion of all, lies the task set for each one,—the securing to every soul the natural opportunity denied by the whole industrial system, both of land and labor, as it stands to-day. This is the goal for all; and by whatever path it is reached, to each and every walker in it, good cheer and unflagging courage, and a leaving the way smoother for feet that will follow, till all paths are at last made plain, and every face set toward the city we seek!

Messrs. Roberts Brothers' Publications.

www.ingramcontent.com/pod-product-compliance
Lightning Source LLC
Chambersburg PA
CBHW080522030426
42337CB00023B/4598